Juan's Story

A True Story

Jacqueline Boatwright

Ps 36 & 37 — Salvation, good
Also read Hebrew 4:16 (notes in Larry's bible)
we can confidently approach the throne
knowing that our prayers & petitions
are welcomed & desired by our heavenly
Father

Juan's Story

PUBLISHED BY
JACKIE BOATWRIGHT ENTERPRISES
P.O. BOX 1821
LITHONIA, GA 30058

Website address: anthonydejuan.com
jackieboatwright.com

Scripture taken from the
New King James Version, Copyright 1982

ISBN 978-0-9725295-1-8

Printed in the United States of America
2007 – Revised Edition

In Dedication

I dedicate this book to my loving mother, Coriene Boatwright. I am so happy that your spirit taught me how to forgive from my heart.

My friends Shelia and Wayne Scarber, Debbie Williams, Frances Burwell, Kevin Bowles, Dot Sapp, Jennifer Taylor, Theracia Prescott and Shirley Newton, your friendship has not wavered and I thank you for that.

To Richard Ingram, thank you for your patience, your unselfishness, your dedication to my cause and giving of your time and expertise. You are one of the most wonderful men I have ever met. I will never forget you, and all you have done for my family and me.

To Greg Rickabaugh, thank you for writing such beautiful stories about my baby and all that we have endured.

The same goes for Timothy Cox, I appreciate you.

To Phil Wasson, thanks for giving 911 the heads up on Juan and for your editing contribution to this book.

To the Augusta, GA, Fire Department, Engine Company 18, Juan is still your baby.

To the Rural Metro Ambulance, EMT's and Paramedics, you did a super job at saving Juan's life, twice.

To the Augusta/Rural Metro 911 dispatchers, you are appreciated by the Boatwright Family.

To my brothers, and my sisters, thank you for your support.

To Adrian and Dereck, I love you both with all my heart.

To the nurses that took such wonderful care of Juan I truly hope that God Bless each of you in a special way.

To the television and radio media that gave us such gracious coverage, especially Leon Moore, thank you.

To P. Kone, my heart will always be open to you for I could never repay you for everything you have brought into our lives. Thank you.

To my "bestest friend" for allowing me a chance to know that my heart still has room for love, crazy laughter and a card game or two every so often. Also thank you for allowing me to mess up your humorous jokes, when I am always trying to tell them to others. I love you and I always will.

To my Pastor, Alan Webb and Church Family, Johnson Chapel Baptist, thank you for loving us spiritually.

To my sheep, HisWay Christian Church Family, thank you for allowing me to serve as your pastor and shepherd. I love each of you dearly.

To Sgt. Ian Ketterer and the brave men and women of his unit. Thank each of you for reading Juan's Story and seeing God in action while fighting in Iraq. Thank you for trusting Christ in spite of your plight.

To all those who said prayers or sent kind words, although I may not have called your name, please know that I deeply appreciate you for all you have done, given, or said to help us along the way.

And last but most certainly above all things here on earth, My Lord and Savior Jesus Christ, thank you for looking beyond my faults and seeing my needs.

Forever,
Jackie

To

Robin Henderson Danforth

Thank you.

May you forever rest in peace.

I Am Woman

Being a woman is the best thing that could have ever happened to me. I learned through countless trials and tribulations that loving me, respecting me, protecting me, and being the best me I could be was the best thing I could do for me.

The hardest time of my life brought true meaning to the old gospel adage, "joy comes in the morning." I have learned to be grateful and appreciative to the things and people in my life that I often took for granted. More than that, I realized that to succeed in life I had to stop negative patterns, stop doing hurtful things to myself and to others.

Learning and understanding my womanhood was a great challenge. Appreciating it was even more of a challenge. After being devastated in a past relationship, I had to find ways to heal my pain and to love those who, for some unknown reason, chose to hurt me. I realized that sometimes you outgrow people, things, and even situations. I decided to be happy. I refused to allow situations, people, or things to interrupt my happiness.

I truly understand my empowerment as a woman, a single mother, a lover, and a friend. I decided to do only what is expected of me, not what others expect of me. I allow myself to laugh, take life slowly and enjoy the simple pleasures that for so long I have rushed by.

I am forever thankful for God's grace and his mercy. So many times when I cried and felt all alone it was that grace and mercy that kept me strong and gave me the extra boost I needed to get through another day. I am stronger than ever in my faith, because I know it gives me hope for tomorrow. My family is a priority, for it keeps me grounded and gives me reasons for setting and achieving goals.

By loving my self I have definitely increased my ability to give and receive love. I have learned to take care of me physically, mentally and emotionally. I've educated my self and embarked on a mission. Yes, I have been dumped, and physically, and verbally abused, yet I still love and appreciate the black man. I know that even though I love my children, my family, and my man, happiness is an individual thing. I have made mistakes with relationships; however, throughout the mistakes, I know I did my best. I will not allow the ugly to stop me from seeing the beauty in what could be, if the right two people connect.

Many times my fears stopped me from reaching my success by undermining my dreams, hopes, and aspirations. I now take those same fears and allow them to activate my efforts to expedite my potential to succeed. The pains and heartaches I suffered from being brokenhearted have become pains and aches of wisdom and courage to do better, be better, want more and have more. I truly understand who I am, and it is me and only me who make me what I am. My courage lies deeply embedded in my heart and soul, fertilized by suffering, pains, healing wounds, and my greatest fears. My empowerment is what shapes and molds me as a woman to be a great mother, a great friend, and a great lover.

I have spent so much time not knowing, not growing, not understanding, and not being understood. Today I stand proud and tall, thankful for the good and the bad, the wrong and the right. I promised me to be consistent with my courage and to not spend the next year doing the same thing I did the year before. I promised me that I was going to reach a little further, seek a little harder, speak a little louder, and listen a little more carefully.

The woman in me will not allow me to give up or give out, not because I was hurt, but because I was hurt; not because I was angry, but because I was angry. I hope one can understand how needless fears and scars can, if not controlled, gain complete control of your destiny.

My inner strength allows me to reach out to others and encourage them to live beyond their front doors, to help them create in themselves today the people they will be tomorrow. Be true to yourself first. I truly believe God gave us all a gift or calling; we have to reach inside and find it, live it, breathe it, believe it, and become it.

I have been faced with many bad situations and had to make the decision to face it or run away. I decided to put my gloves on and fight for the chance to elevate my life. Running away from any situation does not solve it or help it, instead running only adds fuel to the flame. I now know that nine times out of ten almost every situation could have been conquered; if I had taken the time to think, subdue my fear, or slow my anger.

I often dream and I am proud to be a dreamer, if it were not for my dreams, I could not visualize my goals. I teach my children that it is okay to dream, just wake up, and make it a reality. I teach my children to be thankful and pray because your spirituality keeps you running on the right track in life.

I have been up and I have been down so low that I didn't think I could muster the strength to get up and get going again. I opted to reach toward the little voice in me that encouraged me not to stay down, but to get up and run wide open. If I wanted to cry along the way, I cried. If I wanted to scream, I did that, too. Whatever it took to make my running not be in vain, I did.

I take pride in reaching back to enrich others through my obstacles, trials, joys, and heartaches. It feels comforting to know that you are not alone in your struggles, and when you hear the plight of others you realize your fight was not a war, only just a battle.

My womanhood is God's way of telling me I made you strong, proud, smart, and faithful. Being a woman takes all of these qualities and much more. My true beauty lies in my heart, my giving, and in my spirit. It lies in sharing, in my caring, in my reaching, and in my teaching. I am proud to be a woman.

Chapter 1

September 9, 2001, started out as a typical Sunday morning. I was getting ready to go to church. I decided to leave Juan, my fourteen month old son at his daycare center. Juan was very active, and after a period of sitting in one place, he became agitated. How in the world could I have ever known that this day would change my life forever?

I got dressed and played one of my gospel CDs, watching in awe and spiritual laughter as Juan danced on his little feet and clapped his hands, moving to the beat of the music.

"Go, Juan! Go, Juan!" I chanted and praised God along with him.

He was such a beautiful little boy, with perfectly rounded eyes that were so dark that my Mom said, "They look like deep, dark holes in his head." He had two little teeth in the top of his mouth and a matching pair at the bottom. When he smiled I saw his dimples. In complete joy at his rejoicing, I reached out, grabbed him, and gave him a great big hug and kiss.

Suddenly I remembered that the bathtub water was running. I raced to the bathroom to turn the faucet off. I called to Juan, and he came running. He loved to take a bath and splash water everywhere, including my face.

After his bath, I rubbed his little body down in lotion; I could not help stealing a kiss every so often. His soft tiny face and hands tasted like honey, and the more kisses I gave him, the more I wanted to give.

"You've got some sweet kisses, Juan," I told him, and he always answered with the one phrase that he could articulate clearly, "Thank you!" That always got him a great big hug.

I called to Dereck, my twelve year old, "Are you ready yet? It's time to go."

I loaded Juan into his car seat, and we headed a few houses down to his daycare center. His little eyes stared at me with a look that defined everything a few hours later. I rang the doorbell, stealing Juan's sweet kisses as I waited for Maria to answer.

Maria had kept Juan ever since he was about three months old. I met her through a woman at Juan's pediatrician's office. When she told me the location of the day care center where her baby was being kept, my ears perked up. We live on the same street, I thought. She gave me the address and telephone number. The next day I went to see the place. It was clean, and other children were being dropped off as Maria was giving me a tour. She handed me forms to complete and showed me her state license. I liked her.

Maria was a young woman in her late twenties. Throughout her caring for Juan we had many great conversations. Sometimes when I picked Juan up, she and I stood in her driveway talking for about an hour. She had three boys of her own; they all seemed to adore Juan. They often followed us to the car, playing with him as I loaded him in his car seat.

Maria's husband, Monté, was a big, friendly guy, he helped Maria care for the children she kept. I remember times when I called back to the daycare to check on Juan after dropping him off, Monté was watching the children. I thought that was interesting that he had the patience for small children.

He noticed my being anxious about his caring for my Juan, and he would say, "Jackie, Juan is fine, I got everything under control."

"Where is Maria?" I asked.

He would say she was at the grocery store or was gone to get her hair done. He was an adult and he was a part of their business, so what was I so worried about?

As Maria opened the door with outstretched hands, she said to Juan, "Come here boy."

His little arms quickly and tightly grabbed me around my neck. She pulled him away and told him they were going to wake up her boys. I could hear him crying as I walked back to the car. I paused as I reached for the latch to open my car door. A part of me for some unknown reason started to go back in and get him. I decided I would let him stay convincing myself that he would eventually calm down. That decision changed everything for my family and me.

I got in the car and drove to South Carolina for church. As Dereck and I walked through the church door, I saw babies everywhere, and for some strange reason Juan's face would appear on their bodies. I felt a little strange, but told myself I was just missing him. At one point in the service, I heard a baby crying. The crying sounded so much like Juan that I asked if I could hold the baby. I wished in the deepest part of my heart that I had brought him with me, my longing was so strong. I could hardly wait for the service to end.

We sat there as the pastor gave his soul-stirring message titled "It's Your Move." I felt the presence of God inside me, and my soul was filled with joy. The message was about how God is waiting to help us whenever we ask.

The service neared its end so I leaned over and whispered in Dereck's ear, "We are going to stop for ice cream on the way home." That statement woke him up. He had slept through most of the service.

We left from the store eating our ice cream. I told Dereck that I could not wait to get Juan. I pressed on the gas pedal and focused my attention on getting home. My cellular telephone rang. I answered it and saw my message-waiting icon come into the display pad.

"Hello," I said.

It was Delma, Maria's sister. She and I had also become friends. We occasionally went out together and talked on the telephone a lot. We had been playing telephone tag for the past week or so, and her call surprised me.

"Well, you can finally return my calls, huh? Are you at home?" I asked.

She replied, "No, I am at Fort Gordon."

"I guess you want me to come and pick you up?"

"Jackie, this isn't a pleasant call." she said.

My heart fell deep and hard into my stomach as I humbly asked, "What have you all done to my baby?"

"Where are you?" she asked.

"I am on my way home from Edgefield; I was at church. What has happened to Juan?"

"Just come to Eisenhower Hospital as soon as you can."

"Is he alive?" I asked. Complete silence came, and I lost it. I kicked and screamed. The car swerved.

"Oh, my God! Oh, my God! My baby! Why did I leave my baby?" I screamed aloud in the car.

I placed the telephone back to my ear. I could hear her asking me to calm down and reminding me I was driving. I begged her to tell me about Juan, but she would not. I hung up the telephone, and I wept from the inner most parts of my soul.

I felt as though my body were being forcefully crushed, and it hurt

4

me like no other pain I'd ever felt. I began placing calls to family members to let them know that something had happened to Juan. As I tried to regain control, I looked over at Dereck, and the fear in his eyes made me realize I needed to get help, because I was losing it.

It had begun to rain as we approached Augusta. Coupled with my tears and my heartache, I lost all sense of direction. I dialed 911.

I was crying so hard that my words were muffled and broken.

Finally the operator told me, "Ma'am, I can't understand you; stop crying and tell me what is wrong."

As I attempted again to ask the 911 operator for a police officer to drive me to Eisenhower Hospital, I glanced up, and in front of me was a patrol car. I pulled up next to it. I felt weak and numb. I asked Dereck to go inside and get the officer.

As the policewoman approached the car, I shared with her the telephone call I received about my baby, and I asked her to drive me to the hospital where he was.

She asked, "Who placed this call to you, ma'am?"

Unable to respond, I pressed the redial button on my telephone and handed it to her. After a short conversation, she asked me to park my car and get in the car with her. I took off my high-heeled shoes and ran in the rain to get into the patrol car. Once I was in the back of the police car, my head became so heavy I could barely hold it up. I could taste my salted tears. My body continued to ache and feel numb. My imagination took over. What could have happened to him? Was he shot? Was he run over with the car? What?

My thoughts led me to call Maria's home with hopes that one of her children would answer and tell me what happened. My mother had this saying that children and old people are very honest. I prayed that this would be the case and I would learn what happened to Juan.

5

I listened in anticipation of each ring. A man's voice said, "Hello."

"Monté, what has happened to Juan? You can tell me, because I am not driving now, and I need to know what happened to my baby."

"Is this Jackie?" the voice on the other end said.

"Monté, you know this is me. Tell me what is wrong with Juan," I said.

"This is not Monté, this is the police investigator," answered the voice.

I screamed, "Oh my God, what is wrong with my baby? Tell me what happened."

He replied, "I can't, ma'am. Just get to Eisenhower as soon as you can."

I began to kick and scream all over again. I grabbed hold of Dereck, and I wept until we got to the hospital.

Upon our arrival, the officer came around to open the door. I quickly grabbed my purse and shoes and ran into the emergency room, asking anyone who looked as though they worked there, "Where is my baby?"

A woman sitting at the desk said, "You must be Ms. Boatwright. Come with me."

I kept asking her to tell me what happened to my baby. Her replies remained constant, "The doctor will come and tell you in a moment. Just wait here." I could tell by the look in her eyes that it was not good news.

A few moments later the doctor entered and sat next to me. He started to explain to me what had happened to Juan. "It appears your son has suffered a near-drowning accident from falling into a bucket of mop water containing bleach. He has been without a pulse for more than an hour, but we have managed to get a heart-beat. It is not a strong one right now, but we have one."

The only thing that mattered to me was seeing him.

"Can I see him?"

"Sure," he said, "but he has tubes in him, so let me warn you."

Gaining my composure, I entered the room. I could not see my son for the many white coats that stood closely around his bedside. Everything seemed to move and sound as though they were in slow motion. The doctors and nurses peeled back one by one to reveal Juan lying on the bed. I could feel the numbness running full speed up my legs until they felt as though they were not there, and I collapsed. I was quickly brought back to my feet by two of the doctors who asked if I was okay. I slowly walked toward the bed and grabbed my baby. His little body felt like a block of ice, he was not moving, and he looked and felt stiff. I laid my head next to his cheek and told him repeatedly how sorry I was for not taking him to church with me. I wept as my heart pounded in agony.

The doctors pulled me up, saying they had to get him prepared for transport to the Children's Medical Center. I stood outside Juan's room, and I asked the nurse if I could speak to Maria. For some reason, I felt no anger or malice toward her, and I wanted to tell her so. The nurse told me that she was sedated and in another room. We were interrupted by the transport team bringing Juan out of the room.

The ambulance ride from Eisenhower to the Children's Medical Center was just as unbelievable to me as was everything else that had happened. What was going on? Why was this happening to me? Was Juan going to live through this tragedy, and if not, how was I going to live without him?

The paramedics rushed Juan into the hospital. I walked alongside the stretcher and held his little hand, telling him, "Mommy is here, sweetie. You hold on." I held his hand until the paramedics took him through the double doors. I leaned against the wall trying to gain the strength to stand, but my body slid slowly down to the floor. There I sat and wept. The inside of my body felt hollow and cold. I sat and cried until I was able to muster the courage to get myself up and go to the Intensive Care Unit.

I sat in the chair in the corner of Juan's room in the ICU watching closely as the doctors raced to get him stabilized. I saw them take a blower heater and place it under the sheet that covered him in an effort to bring his body temperature back up to normal. They had to connect him to a ventilator because he could not breathe enough on his own to sustain his life. They began to insert needles into various areas of his body. I hurt so much for him. For the first time in his life, I could not kiss his booboo and make him feel better or say anything to make him feel better. I had to stand back, watch, and pray, that somehow or some way he did not feel the trauma he was going through.

His eyes remained closed, as though he did not want to see what was going on. Seeing that image reminded me of when I was a little girl and had to get a shot. I thought that if I closed my eyes it would not hurt as much. I imagined Juan closing his eyes, as I did, with hopes of not feeling the pain.

My prayers were interrupted when Cheryl, Juan's father's wife, entered the room. During the last conversation Cheryl and I had, she told me that she wanted nothing to do with my son. I often wondered how a woman who is a mother could make such a cruel statement. Her telling me such a thing told me that she had a heart of stone. I vowed never to allow her to be alone with him, because I believed in my heart that she would hurt him. I often prayed to God to give me the strength to forgive her. I had definitely accepted her feelings for my son, but her audacity to be in his room at this time was not acceptable to me. How dare her stand in his room as he lay there fighting for his life?

"Get her out of here!" I yelled.

The doctors and nurses hurriedly pushed her into the hallway, asking her to leave. When Juan's father, Anthony, entered the room, I could see the look of hurt on his face. We were not getting along prior to my getting pregnant, and after he walked away two months into my pregnancy, we were not exactly on speaking terms. To add insult to injury, he had gotten married when I was eight months pregnant.

For a brief moment, we seemed to be on the same page about Juan. He walked over, and I could see the look of hurt on his face as he looked at his son, but that lasted about as long as that statement. He started to blame me and call me names. He accused me of allowing anything to happen to Juan.

Bitterness for Anthony crept in, but I refused to allow it to make me lose my focus on my son. I walked to Juan's bedside, and I began to pray. A part of me was glad that Anthony was there, but a deeper part wished that he was not, because of the horrible things he was saying.

As time passed, I would have to walk to and from the bathroom, passing through the waiting room where Cheryl would be sitting. She looked at me with what seemed to be a smirk on her face.

I could not understand how she expected me to accept her being at the hospital after she told me the way she felt about Juan. In my heart, I felt she wished the worst for him. My emotions took over, and I stopped.

"Cheryl, you made it perfectly clear about the way you feel about Juan. He is in there fighting for his life. I want this time to be alone with my baby, because I do not know if this is the last time we will have together. If you do not mind, I truly wish you would leave. I have to come through this area, and to see you here makes me sick to my stomach. Please give me this time with my son," I pleaded to her.

She responded, "I am not here for you and your baby; I am here for my husband."

Satan knows what buttons to push. Please know that I am not glorifying him, just acknowledging how, if I was not careful, he could easily take my focus off my son, and he did. I walked around the corner only to remove my high heels and pantyhose and come back to the waiting room. My anger had gotten the best of me, and I lost control. I began to hit her, dragging her off the couch onto the floor. My mother, sister, and other family members rushed in and pulled me off of her.

"How can she even be here?" I yelled. "I am praying for my baby to live, and she is praying for him to die!"

As she screamed for Anthony to come to her side, he rushed in. He saw the anger that her being there had caused, but he refused to ask her to leave. I cried for my son. How could I have allowed her to take my focus? As I went back to Juan's bedside, I asked God to help me look over her presence and to keep my attention on Juan.

The next several hours were very critical. The lead doctor was telling me that it was not looking good. He said Juan's right lung was beginning to develop air pockets and to harden. They needed to put a tube in to let the air out. I watched as they cut him without giving any sort of anesthetic to numb his pain. I prayed God would take the pain away from him.

The police investigator had arrived and waved his hand to get my attention because he wanted to ask me questions concerning my son's accident. I told him as much as I could, with the information that had been given to me.

My cellular telephone rang constantly as the news about my son spread. Many of those who called were not sure what to say. The hours quickly passed and Juan's fight seemed to get harder, my fears were at an all-time high. I looked to the doctors for some magic words or medicine that would make the tragedy disappear and we could go home.

The next day brought forth more heartache. I placed a telephone call to my good friend Robin. Her telephone rang and rang, and then her voicemail answered. I opted not to leave a message, but instead to give her a call later. I learned of Robin's death after I received a call later that afternoon from another friend offering prayers for Juan and condolences for Robin.

I was hurting all over again. Robin had been diagnosed with leukemia about a year before. She was on sick leave from her job. We would pray for her healing, and she would always reassure me that she was going to beat the cancer that had so unexpectedly invaded her body. She told me that one day while she was eating lunch, one of her teeth just fell out. It was through her dentist that she learned that she carried the horrible disease that robbed her of her young life. I knew that Robin would have been right there with me through all of this, but she was gone, too. I wept for my loss. I truly loved her, and I knew she was one person I could count on for strength. I ached that she would not be able to help me through what I was going through.

I lay awake all night afraid that if I fell asleep I would open my eyes to more painful news. My staying up all night did me no good. The morning brought with it more shock and pain. I stood at my son's bedside with my gaze glued to the television set in total disbelief as the World Trade Center crumbled after terrorists flew two airplanes into it. What in the world was happening? Had the world come to an end and,

I was not informed?

The connection I felt to those in the World Trade Center Buildings was strong. Just like them, I did not see what was coming. I shared the pain of losing or almost losing someone you love dearly as the tragedy ripped my heart into pieces. I, too, felt the disillusion and the vacant disgust. I held on to Juan, and I wept for those people, their families, and our country.

Later that day my niece drove me home to pack some clothes and other personal items. I unlocked my door and hesitated because I knew everything was just as I had left it on Sunday morning. I scanned the den floor and saw Juan's toys lying around the room. My breaths shortened.

"You can do this," I told myself. I rushed down the hallway, and more toys came into my view. I grabbed anything I could out of my drawers and stuffed them into my bag. I turned as I packed and pressed the message button on my telephone. I froze in place. The voice was Robin's.

"Hey Jackie, I was just calling to check on you. The police called me about the baby. Something happened, and they cannot find you. I want to know if you are all right. Let me know if you need me. Call me. I will be around."

I literally choked. The combination of Juan's things and hearing Robin's voice was too much. I had to get out of my own home. I rushed outside to find relief. I got into the car.

"Are you okay?" my niece asked.

"I am okay. Drive me to Maria's house," I said. I had to see her. I had to hear her say she was sorry and to let her know that I forgave her. As I rang the bell my heart raced. Her husband came to the door and invited me in.

12

"Where is Maria?" I asked. Before he could answer, she came from down the hallway with tears in her eyes.

"I am so sorry, Jackie," she said. I held out my arms and embraced her.

"I forgive you," I said. I asked her to tell me what happened to Juan.

She explained, "I had mopped the kitchen floor and was going to mop the bathroom floor. I went to the bathroom, and Juan was there behind me. I came back to the kitchen and he was in the play area, playing with the toys. I went back to the bedroom, and he was not there, but I did not think anything of it because he was playing with the toys. Delson came and knocked on my door and said, 'Mom I think Juan has drowned in the bucket of mop water.' At first I panicked, but then I started doing CPR on him, and Monté called 911. I could bear to hear no more. I told her that if she wanted to come to the hospital, it was okay with me

I got back to find that Juan was still fighting. I sat down next to my mother, laid my head on her shoulder, and wept. A few hours later a woman entered my son's room and asked if she could speak with me. We headed to the consultation room. She introduced herself and told me she was with the Department of Family and Children Services.

"It is a formality, Ms. Boatwright, that we open a case concerning your child." The news sickened me.

"Why are you investigating me? I caused no harm to my child. He was at his daycare," I insisted.

"Well, it is our policy to open a case on the parents when things like this happen," she said, placing a form in front of me. "I need you to sign here saying that you will not allow Ms. Anderson to watch your children anymore."

That was one of those no-brainers. I had not done anything to my child, but here I was defending my character as mother. I signed and was relieved it was over, so I could go back and be with Juan.

I was saddened that because Juan's accident I could not attend Robin's funeral. I still wanted to say good-bye to her. I had a friend drive me over to the funeral home where her body was. I stood in the long line of people waiting to say their good-byes to her. My mind reflected on the times we spent together. She was a kind woman, always giving of herself. She put together my baby shower and brought food over when I came home from the hospital with Juan. She was a perfect example of a true missionary. We spent many times in crazy laughter.

As I approached her casket, I felt joy in my heart, for she looked very pretty and her face presented a peaceful smile. Not wanting to upset the tone of the room, I rushed outside, holding my tears until later. I loved her very much and was feeling so many regrets, for it felt as though our time together was not long enough. I only hoped I said I love you enough to her.

I was walking out of the children's hospital one day when I ran into a young woman and her baby. He was in a wheel-chair and had a tracheotomy tube in his throat. This is a device that is placed in a persons throat to open their airway. The nurses and doctors referred to the tube as a trache, therefore I will do the same throughtout this story. It was there to assist him with his breathing, like Juan's. I approached her as my heart went out for her and her baby. I asked her his name. She told me his name was Darren.

"Hey there, big guy," I said, gently stroking his forehead. He did not move.

"What happened to him?" I asked.

"He choked on a piece of popcorn and lost oxygen to his brain almost two years ago," she replied.

Like her son, she was wheelchair bound. In addition, she had no legs. Her strength and her love for her son encouraged me that I could take care of Juan.

"The doctors wanted me to give up on my baby, but I refused. They thought because I have no legs that I would not be able to take care of him. But I proved them wrong," she said.

We exchanged telephone numbers. We would call to check on each other's children.

People visiting Juan brought with them various rumors of stories from the local paper. I had been hearing comments from friends who had read in the paper, articles about Juan's accident. They told me about a story that Maria did not have a license. I needed to know if it was true. I thought I had remembered her showing me a license on my first visit to her center. I also wanted to tell how I felt about Juan's accident because many of the things I was hearing had begun to bother me.

I called the newspaper and asked for the name of the man who had written the articles. After a brief conversation, he asked if I would do a story with him, I told him that I would, on the condition that he gave God credit for my son's surviving. I met Greg, the newspaper reporter, in the hospital lobby. He looked young and it crossed my mind that he may not have the experience to write a fair story. He assured me that he would write the story as accurate as he possibly could.

I shared with him my feelings and what Maria told me had happened. I really and truly, wanted everyone to know that I was not angry and that I did not hate Maria for what happened to my son. All I wanted was to focus on Juan, my faith, and hopes that God would provide us with a miracle.

Later that day, the lead doctor and his team of residents made their morning rounds. As the lead resident gave her report, I listened in shock as I knew that a lot of what she was saying was not consistent with what I saw.

"I don't have a lot of faith in this team," I said, interrupting the report. I was hurting and everything that was coming out of her mouth was negative.

"Calm down, my baby," my mother said as she patted me gently on my back.

This statement obviously upset the lead doctor, as he responded, "If you don't think this is a good team, you can take him somewhere else." The lead doctor was an African American with salt-and-pepper hair. His arrogance was not helping the situation.

My mother quickly subdued my anger. "Baby, they are doing the best they can. Just pray."

I walked out of the room. As the days passed on, it seemed as though the doctors' interest in treating Juan began to lessen. Their lack of concern angered me because I knew deep inside that their reason of loss interest was about money. I was self-employed and without health insurance. I had been sent a bill for almost $6,000 within the first three days of Juan's hospital stay. What was I going to do with medical bills as excessive as Juan's had become? I knew I could not worry about money at that point. I had to keep my focus on Juan.

The lead doctor asked me to come into the consultation room to discuss Juan. He told me, "Juan is brain dead, and he is not going to ever recover or get any better than what you see now."

I thank God for giving me the strength to stand up for my baby. Once I saw that the doctors were giving up, I decided that I was going to go with God. I had always prayed, and believed, and now I stood in a situation where those beliefs and prayers were all that I had to hold onto.

I told the Dr. Pearson-Shaver, "Thank you for your report, but I have decided to wait for another report from another doctor. You don't mind if I wait do you?"

He asked, "Who is this doctor?"

I looked him directly in his eyes and I said, "Doctor Jesus."

He dropped his head as I walked out to return to Juan's room.

My decision to go with God reminded me daily that the war had just begun. I knew it was going to take every ounce of my strength and then some to stay on the battlefield.

Each doctor on Juan's team had a story to share with me about having to make the decision to remove a family member from life support. It appeared that way, anyway. They tried their best to convince me that pulling the plug on my son was the best thing to do. I often asked myself if they were asking me to pull the plug on him because there was truly no hope, or was money the true reason they were trying so hard to convince me?

One doctor told me he had to pull the plug on his grandmother. "It was the best thing for us to do because of her condition," he said.

"I am sorry about your grandmother. How old was she?" I asked.

"She was ninety-one," he responded.

"I am sure she lived a good life, but my baby has just begun his life, and I want him to live." I replied.

One day a nurse pulled me to the side and told me that I was doing the right thing. She told me that the lead had made the decision to pull the plug on his daughter after a boating accident, and that he was not partial to children being on ventilators. She went on to say that they had suggested to the higher administration that he needed more time before coming back to work, but that fell on deaf ears.

I was shocked at how my interpretation of hospitals was about saving lives, and all the doctors that were treating Juan were asking me to end his life. I loved him and I refused not to give God an opportunity to help me.

One morning I became fed up with the blatant lack of interest in Juan's care. I asked the lead doctor directly, "Is this about money?"

Of course, he denied that money was an issue. "Ms Boatwright, we are going to treat Juan to the best of our ability," he said.

I reminded him of his oath as a doctor to care for my son regardless of our financial capabilities. I told them, "You all need to relax, open you hearts and minds, and allow my God to get in you, so he can heal Juan through you."

School had started back for Dereck. I was faced with the task of getting him ready and taking him to school every day. My mother wanted to take him home with her but I could not bear the thought of having him out of my sight, even in the care of my mother. Each time I looked at him, I could see he really did not understand what was happening in our lives. One morning, after I had just come back from taking Dereck to school, I was approached by the hospital social worker. She told me that one of the nurses on the ICU floor told her I was not sending Dereck to school. The enemy was again trying to break me down. I stood poised and shared.

"Ma'am each and every morning, I get up and take my son to school. I don't know which nurse told you different. Not only do I take him to school, but I have been leaving everyday going to pick him up. We have been living at this hospital for weeks now. Why don't you call the school and ask if my son has not been attending?" I said.

"I am sorry Ms. Boatwright, maybe there is been a some miscommunications," she responded.

I could not believe she would even approach me without at least calling the school to find out if the information she had received was true.

My faith level was at an all-time high, I do not think the nurses and doctors understood me. Rumors had begun to circulate around the unit that I was in denial of Juan's condition. The nurses would carry on conversations about my mental status as though I was not in the room. Two nurses were talking when I overheard one of them say that I was refusing to accept that Juan was not going to live, and that I was losing my mind. Sometimes I would respond by telling them I was crazy all right, crazy about my God and about my baby, and I was not letting go of either of them.

The more negativity I heard, the more I prayed. I would go to the chapel in the hospital and cry out to God to save Juan's life. Each night I sat up watching and hoping for a miracle from God, that God would show up and make them see that all I believed in was real.

As my faith grew, so did my strength.

I remember sitting in the consultation room feeling broken and weary as Juan was once again in a code ninety-nine. I found out that this was a term used by the Children's hospital medical personnel when Juan needed medical attention immediately.

My mind was racing in every different direction. My fears were trying desperately to overcome my faith. Negative thoughts of life insurance money and being free of the responsibility of caring for a small child crept into my mind. Satan was trying to trap me. Realizing this was a great test of my faith, I immediately began to pray and rebuke Satan in the name of Jesus Christ.

"I want Juan!" I said.

Within a few minutes, I heard a knock on the door; it was the doctor telling me that Juan had stabilized. I thanked God for stepping in on time and for knowing my heart.

One night I told God, "Lord I want you to know that I trust you. I am going to sleep in the consultation room, and you and your angels need to watch over Juan."

When I awoke, I found the nurses and doctors standing around Juan's bed and shaking their heads in total confusion. As I got closer to his room, I looked up at his monitor to see his little heart beating 258 beats per minute and climbing. Oh my God, I thought. As they walked out one by one, I knew that it was up to me to make the next move. I asked the nurse to lower his bed so I could lie down next to him and pray.

I held his head in my arms, and I began to pray. "Lord, I know that you can help my baby. You are the same God today as you were when you took care of the Hebrew boys. The same God that protected Daniel in the lion's den, that raised Lazarus from the dead, made blind see, the lame walk and the dumb talk." I reflected on the message I had heard September 9 at church. I began to repeat that day's text. "It's your move. God, it's your move."

I lay in the bed crying and holding onto my baby. I noticed a nurse walking into my son's room and stumble backward with a startled look on her face. She turned pale white.

"What's wrong?" I asked as I sat up to look at the monitor. His heart rate had dropped to 158 beats per minute.

"Did you give him anything?" I asked.

She replied, "No. I didn't give him anything!"

20

I laid back down next to Juan. I silently began to praise God for what I knew only He could have done. I cried tears mixed with joy and sorrow.

All of a sudden I heard a voice speak in the room. "Hush!" the voice said.

I looked around the room to find no one there but Juan and me.

"I am going to heal that baby."

I knew it was the voice of God. I could feel the presence and a calm come over me. I replied, "God, they say his lungs are severely damaged."

"I am going to fix his lungs," He said.

I asked, "What about his brain?"

"I am going to fix his brain," God replied.

"Lord, you see his heart is racing out of control."

"Hush, I am going to fix his heart too."

Was I going crazy? No, I knew that the Holy Spirit had come to my rescue. I had to keep believing in Him, no matter what happened or how things looked.

The rest of the day brought forth a little more comfort, as Juan seemed to settle down. As I walked down the hallway, my heart hurt, for it finally hit me that all the patients here were babies. The first room held a baby that had been there for about two or three years. His mom and dad visited him each day, along with his two brothers. The nurses would often hold him and play with him, because he had been there with them for a long time.

The second room held a baby I would often see alone throughout the day. I would stand at his door and watch him play with the angels and coo into the air, waving his little hands as he seemed to focus on something or someone above him. He was born with heart problems.

21

Juan was in the center of the ICU. In the next room was a little girl battling cancer. Her mom told me her story. She often come over and inquired about Juan. We exchanged inspirational books and pray for each other's child. She was a strong believer in God too, and her pastor visited on a regular basis.

At the end of the hall was a little boy who also had heart problems. I prayed that God would heal all of these babies along with my Juan.

One night the baby that was alone most of the time went into a code ninety-nine. As the alarms sounded, the nurses and doctors rushed to his room. His parents were unable to be reached. I stood there watching at Juan's door and praying that God would keep him alive for his mother to be by his side.

God heard and answered my prayer. His mother came, and the doctors told her his heart was failing. She sobbed as she went and kissed him good-bye. I wondered if she prayed to God to help him. As I walked toward her, her eyes said it all. If the eyes are truly the entrance to the soul, then hers showed the vast rip that she had just endured.

I asked her if she wanted to pray. She replied, "I am tired of him suffering. I want to let him go."

He lay there until his little heart stopped.

For the hospital, this type of incident was common. They cleaned the room and prepared it for the next baby that would soon occupy it. The family of the baby with cancer moved into his room, because it was larger. Another baby filled the room that they vacated.

A few mornings later as I lay asleep, I was awakened by the screams of a woman. "My baby! No, God, my baby!"

I jumped up in fear, because I had been asleep and was caught off guard. I entered the waiting room somewhat disoriented to find a mother and father screeching in pain from the loss of their baby. Here again, as I watched in pain with them, I found myself holding on to the mother and crying with her for her child.

"Oh, my God," I thought, "I am in the midst of death." I just kept praying harder and harder each day. You see, in the midst of death, I must admit, my fears started to set in. Was Juan next?

I began to recite the twenty-third Psalm. I knew that I had to regain my faith in order to win the battle. I also knew that the Word of God gives us all so many days on this earth. I believe that our lives are already written prior to our arrival. Some people have many days, and others have only a short number of days. I prayed that Juan's life be written with many days. I had to remain focused on my faith. I knew that God can and will do. I needed the strength to wait for God even when there seemed to be no hope.

Because of my renewal of faith, I refused to allow anyone to enter Juan's room with negative thoughts or conversation. Even when his body began to swell, distorting his face, I held on to my faith, and I told him how beautiful he was.

I had received a telephone call that the lead investigator wanted me to come to the police station. When I arrived I was greeted by a tall slender black man.

"Hello, Ms. Boatwright, my name is Major Autry. I appreciate your coming." he said extending his hand to shake mine.

"You are welcome." I responded.

"Please be seated. This gentleman is from the DA's office he is here to tell you of the criminal charges against Ms. Anderson for what happened to your son." he went on to say.

"Please don't send her to jail. I don't think she meant to hurt my child," I pleaded with the investigator.

"This is not your call, Ms. Boatwright, it's ours. We plan to recreate the crime scene to find out what really happened," he said.

The man from the DA's office entered the conversation and began to explain the type of sentence given, for what they wanted to charge Maria with. He said that because my son did not die, there would not be a lot of time they could ask for, but she would definitely do some time if they had anything to do with it.

"Please, I don't want Maria to go to jail," I pleaded again.

The investigator asked if he could show me the type of bucket the water was in that she used to mop the floor.

My throat immediately got full as I softly whispered, "Juan was bigger than that bucket. He could have turned it over." I thought no one heard me.

"We feel the same way, Ms. Boatwright that is why we want to find out if everything happened the way they are telling us it happened," the man from the DA's office said.

The investigator probably could see the look on my face and said, "I see how much this means to you, so I am going to drop it for that reason."

I thanked him and left.

After I left the police station, my thoughts were going back and forth about what happened on September 9. I knew I had to let it go. I didn't think I could bear to hear anything different at that point in time. I was just glad that Juan was alive, and I did not want to focus how or why the tragedy happened to him. After seeing the bucket, I found myself praying diligently and often to make it through my thoughts about what happened.

It was one of the toughest fights with the enemy as everybody around me believed there was more to what was being told about Juan's accident.

One day, as I sat watching television I looked up to find a woman standing at the door to Juan's room. I could see her mouth moving, but I could not hear her, because of her soft-spoken voice.

As I walked to her, she asked, "What is wrong with your baby?" I told her Juan's story. "Why are you so sad?" I asked.

"My baby is in the room on the end, and he is not doing too well." I told her, "You must trust in God."

"Will you pray for him?" she asked.

"Sure," I replied. As I put on the gown and gloves to enter his room, I silently asked God to be with me. "He is so handsome," I said to her. I told her, "Now that you have prayed to God, act as though your blessing has come."

We would go on to find comfort in each other through our conversations. She would often share with me her dreams of my baby and her baby waking up at the same time. What a beautiful dream!

The next morning I received a call from the social worker asking me to come to the business office to sign for payment of the hospital bill. As I rode the elevator down to the first floor, I could not help noticing the eerie feeling that had come upon me earlier that morning. I was not sure of what it meant; I just knew that I did not like it.

I kept saying to myself, "I must go to the chapel and pray." I felt that if I could just pray God would relieve me of whatever it was I was about to encounter. After leaving the business office, I went around the corner to the chapel and I prayed to God asking him to remove whatever negative there was about my feeling. "God please give me some reassurance that Juan is going to be okay," I prayed.

As I rode the elevator back up to the ICU, I felt somewhat better

25

but not totally relieved of this feeling.

I walked into Juan's room, and there was a woman standing next to my mother. Fearing the worst, I asked, "Mom, what has happened?"

"Everything is okay with the baby. This woman is here to see you," my mother replied.

She came around to the side of Juan's bed where I stood and said, "I know that you don't know me, because I don't know you. God woke me up in my sleep last night and told me I had to come tell you that your baby has already been healed, but you have to let go of any anger you have."

I assured her that I forgave Maria days before. I looked at her in awe, because I knew that I had been downstairs praying to God for reassurance of Juan's being okay, and this woman had been standing here with an answer to my prayer. "Who did you come to visit?" I asked.

"You are the only reason I am at this hospital. I traveled more than fifty miles to come here to tell you this information," she answered.

We began to praise God together. We exchanged telephone numbers and she left.

Later that night I called her, and she told me how she found us. She explained, "I don't get the Augusta newspaper, but my mother-in-law does. She was on vacation and asked me to get her mail and toss the newspaper, because by the time she returned home, it would be old news anyway. I had been throwing them all away, when I decided to read the one that had the story on your baby. I felt bad about him and prayed for him. I thought that was all I had to do.

Later that same night, as I tried to sleep, I was literally tossed in my bed. The voice of God told me that I had to get up and go tell you that the baby has been healed. I was unsure about all of this. The next morning, it was on my heart that I had to come there to tell you that your baby has been healed.

My two daughters and I got in the car and headed for our appointment, I passed the road that I needed to turn on. My daughters questioned me. I told them that I had to go tell this woman that her baby is healed. I asked God that if this is what He wanted me to do to please give me some sort of sign. Immediately a song came on the radio about being obedient to God. I knew then that I had to go. Every traffic light that I got to was on green."

I praised God for the timing and for sending this message of confirmation to me.

A few days later I stood at the desk next to Juan's bed as I talked on the telephone. "Oh, my God, he moved his hand!" I said to the nurse.

Her response was one of total disbelief. "That is just a reflex, and I didn't see him move."

As I started to argue with her, Juan raised his little hand again and made a fist.

"There, he did it again!" I screeched.

"Hum," she replied.

"I am not crazy. I know I saw him move!"

Another nurse overhearing the conversation had walked into the room. "You are not crazy, Ms. Boatwright. I saw him move, too."

I embraced her and shed tears of joy as I thanked her. Juan also had started to take breaths on his own. Because of his breathing over the ventilator, the nurse told me doctors had decided to remove his tube to see if he could breathe enough on his own to keep him alive without the ventilator. I waited patiently for the doctor to come.

His arrival was more painful than I had expected. When he walked into the room, he grabbed a chair, propped his feet up, and placed both hands behind his head. "If he doesn't breathe enough on his own, do you want us to let him die?"

I could have punched him. How could he even ask me such a question? "No, do not let him die! You insert that tube back in him, and you let him breathe again!"

Seeing he had upset me, he tried to explain. "We just have to give you all of your options, Ms. Boatwright."

"You listen to me; Juan dying is not an option!"

He left knowing that I was angry. When the moment came for the trial of his breathing on his own, my heart raced wide open as though I were in the Indianapolis 500. While I clung to my friend's hand, the tube was removed.

Juan's oxygen level dropped, the doctor rushed to get the tube reinserted. I crumpled to the floor, briefly losing consciousness. My sight came back, and I was surrounded by nurses.

"Oh, my God!" I cried.

"He is okay," a voice in the crowd said.

Another voice asked, "Do you want me to get the chaplain?"

"Yes," I whispered.

I was being helped to a nearby chair when the chaplain came and knelt next to me. I was desperately hoping that we would pray and remind me of the power of God.

"I am so sorry things aren't going the way you want them to," he said.

I sat there waiting for more, I realized that was it. He had said all he was going to say to me.

"Everybody just leave!" I said, as I got up and walked to Juan's bedside. "Okay, my baby; we are rushing God. He is not ready yet, so we are going to get back on our bandwagon of faith and we are going to wait for Him." I began to praise God as I wiped the tears from my face.

I could not understand why a minister, of all people, would make no attempt to reassure me of my faith in God.

A few weeks before this situation occurred another minister called me on the phone.

He said, "I am going to pray, but remember sometimes even when we pray, things go the other way."

My stomach tightened as I refused to believe that God would confuse me. Why would His word say that the answers to my prayers would be granted if I trusted in Him with all my heart if He was not going to do it?

Just so you know, He is not a God of confusion. His word says that anything we ask in the name of Jesus will be given. He does not second guess the things that He says He will give to us.

Chapter 2

My heart was led to change the way I prayed. I was always taught to say, "Lord if it is your will, do this or do that."

He says He will do what he tells us in the Bible. Adding that phrase leaves room for doubt or lack of faith, so when our blessing doesn't happen, we can say it was not God's will: Or was it truly our lack of faith that was the reason of our not receiving the promises of God?

The word says that "Lord, if it is your will" should be applied to things that we say we are going to do, for example, to go here or to do this, because we can do only what He allow us to do. But everything He says He will do will be done, according to your faith in Him.

The morning would bring new hopes and leave old hopes behind us. Another trip home to get clean clothing and check my mail gave me new hopes. I was shocked to see the amount of my cellular telephone bill.

"Oh, my God, I need this phone. Lord, this is the only way the hospital can contact me when I step outside those doors," I prayed.

I picked up my home telephone and called the cellular company to set up payment arrangements.

"How may I help you?" the voice said. I explained to her all that had happened and the reason why my bill was so high.

"Can you verify the last four numbers of your Social Security number?" she asked. I told her the digits.

"I am sorry, Ms. Boatwright, your cellular phone has been disconnected for nonpayment and because of the amount of the bill, we are unable to turn it back on until we receive payment," she said.

At that moment, my cellular telephone, lying on the table, rang.

"Could you please hold for a second?" I asked. I answered my cell telephone. It was the hospital wanting to know the time of my return, because I needed to sign some documents.

"I'll be back in about a half hour," I said and hung up.

I returned to the line with the cell telephone representative, "Are you sure my telephone is disconnected?"

She angrily repeated all of my account information. "Not only is it disconnected, it has been disconnected for two weeks, and as I told you before, we are not going to turn it back on until we get some money!"

I re-dialed the hospital number and was shocked when I heard, "MCG, how may I help you?"

I thanked the woman at the telephone company for her time. God had again answered my prayers. I returned to the hospital.

The day turned to night I kissed Juan on his forehead "Night, night my sweet baby." I walked over to the cot where Dereck was asleep and kissed him as well.

I sat down and removed my shoes. I began to lie down, and a voice, which I will call the Holy Spirit, from this point on, , said to me, "Get up, Jackie. Get up and go to Juan's bed."

I raced as hurriedly as the tone of the voice.

The voice said, "Rub his foot and watch it move."

I rubbed Juan's foot, and as the voice said." It moved. I backed away from the bed in fear of what was happening.

"God, if this is you, you need to let me know, because I think that I am losing my mind," I said in a low voice, being careful not to let

31

anyone hear me talking to myself.

I walked back to the cot and attempted to lie down again.

"Get up, Jackie. Get up. You are going to miss it! Get up! Get up!"

Again I rushed to Juan's bed to the sound of the voice of the Holy Spirit,.

"Rub his foot and watch it move," he said.

I rubbed his foot, and the foot moved. I began to cry.

"How are you going to tell it, Jackie?" he asked.

"What do you mean?" I said.

"How are you going to tell everybody about all of this?"

"I don't know, Lord, but I am going to make them know that it is you," I replied.

He then said, "I am going to prove to you I am who I am. A nurse is going to come into the room. I am going to have her leave by making the alarms in the next room go off."

As I lay there with my head under the covers, I heard the nurse enter the room. She acknowledged herself by speaking to me. My son's alarm immediately went off and quickly silenced. Just as I thought that it was not going to happen, I heard all of the alarms in the next room go off. The nurse raced out of the room.

"I told you," he said.

What was happening to me?

As the hours rolled by, Juan was still holding on, and I can tell you each day got easier and easier. My pastor and church family, as well as my friends and family, would visit from day to day. One or another of them would break down in tears upon looking at Juan's swollen, tube-filled body. I comforted them, assuring them that he was going to be okay. They could not understand why I was not torn apart with all that was happening.

We walked the floor praying for the other babies and their families. More and more, I began to understand my mission.

My eyes opened to Sunday morning, I heard the voice of God speak to me again.

"Get up and go home and put on the same clothes you wore on the day this happened, I am going to send you to a church," He said.

I immediately got up and went home to get dressed. I did as God asked and put on the same clothing. I drove down the street not sure of which church I would attend. My mind thought of several churches that I had attended or that I knew of.

Each thought brought forth the same answer from the voice of God. "That is not the one," He would reply.

"Lord, I know that you are not going to have me go back to South Carolina to church." I said.

"No," He replied. "I am going to tell you where to go."

"Wherever you send me, let me get something out of the service as well as give something back," I prayed.

I drove around the city, I even pulled into a church parking lot. The voice of God said. "This is not the one."

Along my journey, the car began to pull to the right, almost as if I could not control it. I did not fight as I steered into the church parking lot. I stared at the marquee, it read Methodist.

I quickly questioned God. "God, are you sure this is the right one, I am Baptist?"

"This is the one," He said.

I got out of the car and stood in confusion as to which set of double doors I was to enter. I glanced back at the marquee to check the time of the service. As I turned back around, one of the double doors partially opened.

I walked up the stairs and went inside. I sat down in the sanctuary, my attention focused on the children's Sunday School class. Their lesson was about when God raised Lazarus from the dead.

As the class ended and the teachers asked for questions and comments, I stood and told them about Juan. The two women in the class had read about Juan in the newspaper and asked me to come up to the area where the class was. The man, whom I later found out was the associate pastor, asked me how I found out about their church. I immediately started telling him of the voice of God and what God had said for me to do.

As I conversed with the women concerning Juan, another man entered the room. He was the pastor of the church. I shared with him how I came to their church. After a brief conversation, he asked me to speak to his congregation during the morning worship service. I was totally shocked. I had not prepared a speech. I agreed.

As I told Juan's story, there was hardly a dry eye in the place. I left and returned to the hospital with a new message in my heart and mind. *Obedience is Better Than Sacrifice.* The minister had delivered a soul-stirring message about the time when God had asked Abraham to sacrifice his son Isaac, and Abraham's obedience led to God's sparing Isaac's life.

I drifted off to sleep with unspeakable joy in my heart. I awakened and saw a good friend of mine standing at Juan's bedside.

"Miss Debbie, why didn't you wake me up?" I said to her.

"I knew you were tired, and I thought I would let you sleep," she replied.

I met Miss Debbie, a second-grade teacher, through her membership at my fitness club. She and I had become close friends. We shared many spirit-filled conversations as we walked the treadmill. Whenever people asked me to pray with them, I immediately grabbed her by the arm because I knew she was very close to God.

"So, how have you been doing?" she asked.

"I am fine," I responded.

She always brought me some sort of gift. Her compassion and sincere love for my children and me always touched my heart.

"Jackie, there is a family on the fourth floor that I would like for you to pray with." She told me that the young man was in a three-wheeler accident and had a head injury that left him fighting for his life. They were not expecting him to live.

"Let's go!" I said.

"You do not have to go now; I know you are tired," Miss Debbie said. I assured her it was okay, and we headed to the fourth floor.

When we arrived, the family was crying and broken. The mother and father of the injured man sat huddled together in the hallway. The mother clutched her Bible and sobbed, my heart went out to her. I knelt down, in front of them and I told them the story of Abraham and Isaac. I told them that God did not want their son. He wanted them. I prayed with them and shared in their pain and heartache.

Miss Debbie and I returned to Juan's floor where we said good-bye at the elevator. Before she left she handed me a stack of letters from her second-grade class. They had wrote me heartfelt letters encouraging me to continue praying and believing that Juan was going to be okay.

I could have held on to her forever as she embraced me and said, "I love you."

I kissed Juan softly on his cheek. I took a deep breath to savor his sweet smell. I loved him so much. Night began to fall and my eyes got heavy, I said a prayer to God and drifted off to sleep.

The next morning I awoke to find Juan still holding on. My heart was filled with new hopes for his healing.

The nurses and hospital staff walked in and attended to Juan, I casually asked, "Do you believe in God?" Some of them said, yes, they did believe in God.

One therapist told me he did not believe. "If there is a God; why does he let all these things happen to babies?" he said.

While he examined my son's breathing machine, I immediately asked God to forgive him and to anoint his hands as he worked with Juan.

Later that afternoon God spoke to me again. "Go back to the fourth floor."

I went back to find the family of the young man even more broken than before. I silently asked God for the right words to say to them. The young man's wife was taking the doctor's latest news very hard. I asked her to come into the hallway. My intentions were to give her my shoulder to cry on and to tell her to be strong, that he was going to be okay.

As I embraced her, I asked, "Do you know who God is?"

She replied, "No."

"Well, let me tell you who He is." I said to her. "He is big and bad enough to do anything He wants, and that includes heal your husband."

As we walked to the staircase and sat down, I asked her, "Do you want to be saved?"

With a look of confusion, she did not respond. I told her that her salvation and devotion to God would help bring forth the healing for her husband.

According to the Bible, I said, "All you have to do is to confess your sins and believe that Jesus was raised from the dead, and you will be saved."

She immediately repeated the scripture of salvation, and we embraced with unspeakable joy at her being saved. I told her that her salvation was a daily task that she would have to work at living the life God has intended for her.

I am so glad that God gave me understanding to know, according to the word, all He requests is mere acknowledgment of your sins and of Jesus' living. With this acknowledgment, you will know that you can call upon Him and He will come to your side at any given moment.

I was amazed the young woman did not know that God was waiting to help her; all she had to do was call on Him. We walked back into the waiting room with the rest of her family and shared the good news.

I was truly overjoyed as I walked back to Juan's room praising God for what he had just used me to do. I kept telling myself that I am not worthy of such a great task, but my heart told me that God saw something in me I did not see in myself.

The next morning the social worker approached me about going to the Social Security office to apply for disability for Juan. As my faith had strengthened, I told the man that Juan was not disabled, and I did not want to apply for disability. He looked at me strangely and said that he admired my faith, and he walked out of the room.

I gained an awesome amount of strength that kept coming, and at times I amazed myself with all that I had handled. There were times when things were bad with Juan. I asked myself why I was not crying. I would often attempt to cry and found that I was unable to do so. No tears would fall, instead my heart felt happy and content. For the first time in my life, I truly understood the passage in the Bible that says God will give you strength that surpasses all understanding.

Later that night my pastor and his wife came to visit Juan. I could see the look of fear in my pastor's face. I told him of my faith in God and what I knew God was going to do for Juan. As we prayed for Juan, I prayed for my pastor's strength.

The next day the young man on the fourth floor and his family were on my heart and mind.

When I got to the waiting room, the young man's mother asked me, "Who keeps calling you to come here? You seem to come when we need you."

I began to share with her the voice of God telling me to come. We prayed and I left. Later that night, as I slept, sharp pain in my stomach awakened me. I sat up hoping it would go away. The pain did not stop. Half asleep I walked to the bathroom, and I reached to open the door.

The voice of God said, "You have to go back to the fourth floor."

"But God, it's almost two o'clock!"

He said, "I know, but you have go back. Go put your shoes on."

I walked back to Juan's room, sat down on the cot, and put on my shoes. I picked up my Bible and asked myself what I was going to say to the family.

God said, "Close the book. I will tell you what to say when you get there."

I walked down the long corridor and got on the elevator that led to the fourth floor.

As I stood outside in the fourth floor corridor, I saw the young man's mother and father as they flipped out a blanket, preparing to lie down and rest. They were the only two people awake. I wondered to myself why I was here.

The father looked up and saw me. He rushed out, grabbed my hands, and asked me to tell him what to do because they were saying that his son was not going to make it.

"All I know to tell you is keep praying and trusting in God," I said.

"No, you pray!" he responded, as he grabbed me by the hand, leading me to his son's bedside.

That was the first time that I had actually seen the young man. I could hardly swallow as I looked at his comatose body filled with tubes and simply lying there, just as Juan lay in his bed. I walked to his bedside, reached back, and held his mother's hand as she joined hands with her husband.

I laid my hand on the young man's shoulder and said aloud, "God, I don't know why I am here, but You asked me to come, so have Your way."

I immediately began to weep, but I was aware that the weeping was not my own. All of a sudden, my body began to shiver from the top of my head to the bottom of my feet. As I prayed to God, I started speaking in other tongues and languages. I was frightened but realized that my body was a being used as a vessel by God. I stood in fear and allowed the Holy Spirit to continue.

The father and mother were afraid. The father ran from the room. The mother could only get away the distance of my arm.

I heard the father ask her, "My God, what is wrong with her?"

She replied, "I don't know, but I think she is talking with God."

Finally it was over. I felt weak and drained as we walked back into the waiting area.

As I stood there in tears praising God, I looked to find the mother and father on their knees in front of me asking, "Tell us what we need to do to be saved."

I replied, "Romans ten and nine."

They began to flip through their Bibles to find the scripture, I asked that they close the book and repeat after me. They did and were saved that very moment.

As I walked back down the long corridor leading to Juan's room at ICU, I talked with God.

"Please make this miracle happen. These people were saved according to my faith."

As I reached the door that led to the ICU, I looked into the glass window in front of me that overlooked the parking lot. Because of the lighting, the glass gave a reflection of the long corridor that was behind me. I saw an image walking behind me, and as soon as I saw it, it disappeared into thin air. My fears heightened as I rang the buzzer repeatedly to enter the ICU area. When I finally got back into bed, I lay there unable to sleep. I wondered what all of the events that had happened to me meant. Would people believe me when I told them?

The next morning I called Maria to ask about her insurance carrier. I was shocked to find out that she was not insured. I called the Department of Human Resources to ask if they were aware that she had no liability insurance on the day care business.

"We don't require day care centers that we license to have insurance," the woman on the other end of the telephone said to me.

"You have to be kidding, right? That is totally ridiculous!" I slammed the down on the receiver.

As I thumbed through the Yellow Pages to find an attorney, my attention stopped on the second name that I saw. I dialed the number and asked to speak with an attorney. I briefly explained my situation. He agreed to come to the hospital the next day to meet me.

Sitting down in the chair, I dialed Maria's number again to get the name of her homeowner's insurance.

"It is not in my name, it is in my husband's name," she said.

"It doesn't matter whose name it is in, I just need to know the name of the carrier so I can try to get some help with Juan's medical bills," I said.

"I will ask my husband who it is, because I don't know," she responded.

"Okay," I said and hung up.

She does not have insurance. How can this be? Oh, my God. What am I going to do?

The next day as I sat in the waiting room awaiting the arrival of the attorney, I prayed that everything somehow work itself out. I looked to find a tall, young gentleman coming toward me.

He extended his hand and introduced himself. "My name is Richard Ingram. I am the attorney you spoke with on the phone yesterday."

"Thank you so much for coming," I said, firmly shaking his hand.

"You know, God has to be in this. I have already tried and won a case just like this," he said.

When he spoke of God sending him, my heart was overjoyed with the fact that he knew God. I felt my prayer was answered. He went on to tell me that he would try to find out the name of the homeowner's insurance company.

I asked him if he would like to see my baby. He said yes, and we walked into Juan's room. I could see the compassion in his eyes as he looked around the room and at Juan.

"I am going to do all I can to help you with," he said as he left.

The next few days brought good news. Juan was stable enough to go home!

The doctors told me that I would have to prove that I could take care of him, before I would be allowed to take him home. Just the thought of going home was music to my ears. I believed in my heart that if I took Juan home he would get better. I became like a sponge soaking in every bit of knowledge about his care. I had been the type of person who had a weak stomach, but my love for Juan cured that.

As time progressed and Juan got a little better, we moved out of ICU to the fourth floor. The fourth floor is the next step before going home. Each day brought forth more excitement about the possibility of going home. We had spent more than 30 days in the ICU, and I was ready to go home. I could not believe that it was almost November. The thought of spending Thanksgiving at home was a pleasant one. The feel of my bed and not living out of a suitcase brought joy as well. The transition to the fourth floor went smoothly.

The nurses told me that I had to have a backup caregiver trained to take care of Juan. My mind raced with thoughts of who I ask would to take on such great task. I thought of a close friend of mine. She had always been a good friend to me. She was even there for Juan's birth and was christened as his godmother. She worked as certified nurse's assistant in a neighboring hospital. Almost every day on her way home from work she would stop in and visit Juan. Even if I had stepped away from his room briefly, I knew that she had been there, because of the set of red lips on Juan's cheek where she would plant her kisses. We had met sometime before and became close friends as we shared in each other's joys and sorrows. I called her at her job.

"Hi, girl. This is Jackie. I called to ask a favor of you. The hospital is going to let me take my baby home, but I need a backup person who can help me take care of him to get the state to provide him home nursing care," I told her.

"What would I have to do?" she asked.

"Well, they told me that they would spend the next few weeks

42

training me and my backup caregiver on how to take care of him. Once we demonstrated that we could do the procedures, I could take him home."

"Let me talk to my husband about it and see what he thinks," she said.

"Okay. I will talk with you tomorrow," I said.

I did not have any reason to suspect that he would tell her she could not help me, because he was also christened as Juan's godfather.

Weeks went by and I did not hear from her. My fears set in and I broke down. I was afraid that the doctors were not going to let me bring Juan home. I called my mother.

"Hi, Mom."

"What's wrong my baby? Is Juan okay?"

"Yes, he is doing fine," I said. "They told me I could take him home if I had someone else trained to take care of him."

"That's good."

"I asked my friend, but I have not heard back from her," I said. "Mom, all I want to do is to get him home. I will give up everything to take care of him and to try to get him back up on his feet. Will you please come up here and help me?"

"Sure, baby; you know I will do all I can to help you. Mamma is old now, but I will do all that I can."

"Thank you, Mama," I said tearfully.

A few days later, my friend stopped by and asked if Dereck could go home to spend the night with her son. I let him go. I noticed that she still did not mention an about being a backup caregiver for Juan.

The next morning when she dropped Dereck off at the hospital on her way to work she said. "I asked my husband about what you asked us to do, and he said 'No, No, No, child!' What if something happened? You would blame us."

My heart was sad to think that she assumed I would blame them for anything happening to Juan.

"First of all, my mom has agreed to be my secondary caregiver," I said. "Secondly, I am not taking my baby home to die. I am taking him home to live. If God chose to take him, then why would I blame you? Tell me this: You stood before God, my pastor, and my family saying that you would take on the responsibility of being godparents to my son. What if something had happened to me, what would happen to Juan?"

"We would take him," she said, shyly looking away.

"You can't convince me of that. You don't want to help me with him so I know that you would not take him on your own in his condition."

I think we both knew that the special bond that we once shared had just been severed. Would we ever be the way we were?

I had to stay focused on Juan. He was my baby, and no matter who walked out on him as his mother, I was not going to give up on him. I loved him and if it meant losing those I thought were my friends, then that was a price I would have to pay to help him get well.

The room we occupied on the fourth floor was much roomier than the one at ICU. It resembled a hotel suite. My mother, Dereck and I settled in easily. We had become more relaxed and often found ourselves laughing and cracking jokes. Hamburgers and French fries had been our supper for quite some time, but none of us complained about it.

It was refreshing to finally be around many God-fearing nurses and assistants. Many of them joined hands with me and prayed for Juan. They shared in my hopes for a miracle. I returned to Juan's room one afternoon to find my Bible open to the fifth chapter in the book of

James. My eyes focused on the words.

It said, "Is any sick among you? Let him call for the elders of the church; and let them pray over him, anointing him with oil in the name of the Lord: and the prayer of faith shall save the sick, and the Lord shall raise him up."

I ran out of the hospital and went to the grocery store. I bought some oil so that I could do as the verse said about anointing his head with oil. I had to trust God, because he had brought me to the point where I stood.

We had much to learn and in such a short time. The information at times was confusing because of the medical terms the nurses used during our training. I would often watch in disgust at the look on my mother's face. I had learned to master the terms quickly, but my seventy-five-year-old mother was totally lost. Her lack of understanding stood out as she attempted to demonstrate the techniques. This made me so angry.

One day I snapped, yelling at the nurses who were training her. "You all just stop! This is too much too soon!" I said, running from the room.

I went into the waiting area, sat in a chair, and let my emotions go. I began to blame myself for Juan's accident and for having to put my mother through the task of learning to care for Juan. After about thirty minutes had passed and my self-anger was subdued, I walked back into the room and shared my feelings with the nurses training my mother and me.

"Listen, you are talking over my mother's head. When we get home, we are not going to be talking like this. Put this in terms that she will know exactly what you are saying. Use visual descriptions. Just say it like you know we would say it."

I think the nurses finally understood my frustration. One of the nurses wrote across the chalkboard in Juan's room, Use layman's terms when training.

With our new teaching method, my mother became the Florence Nightingale of the fourth floor. As our going home was quickly approaching, the social worker gave me the name of the nursing company that would assist me with Juan's home care.

"They will be contacting you soon and coming to meet you," she said, handing me the company business card. I placed the card on the table after looking at it. The next day, I shared with two nurse assistants that Juan would be going home soon. I went on to tell them about the nursing company.

"Oh, my goodness," the female assistant said under her breath.

"What do you mean?" I asked.

"I have used that company for quite some time. I am a mother of a vent-dependant child. The nurses hardly ever show up, and they overmedicated my son," she said.

The overmedicating scared me. I called the social worker and shared the information I received from the nursing assistant. "Can you give me the name of another company?" I asked.

"I am sorry, Ms. Boatwright; they are the only company that cares for children on home ventilators," she responded. "I have a personal relationship with the company manager. I will speak with the manager about your concerns and have her come and talk with you before you leave the hospital." I felt a little better.

The next morning, the manager of the nursing company came to visit me. She introduced herself and asked if she could have a moment to speak with me. We walked into the waiting area and sat in the two chairs that overlooked the parking lot. My nerves were on full alert, and as my heartbeat began to speed up. I took a deep breath and listened carefully as she shared her company's history.

"I know that you have heard some horrible things about our company, but those things happened a long time ago. Since I have been manager, things have changed for the better. I promise you, Ms. Boatwright, nothing like that would ever happen to your child if you trust us to take care of him."

Her girl-next-door look and sweet tone reassured me to trust her company to take care of him. My nerves must have been reassured as well, for the beat of my heart had slowed by the end of our conversation.

The next few days were the countdown to November 13, our release day. I ran back and forth between the house and the hospital, trying to get things prepared for Juan to come home. I decided to exchange his room with the room that Dereck slept in. As I moved his crib from the back bedroom to the bedroom up the hall, my mind reflected. Juan had slept in this crib overnight only once; the night before his accident.

I had bought a new Bible and given my old Bible to Dereck. I had taken Juan and placed him in the crib. I sat back on the bed and began to read my Bible.

"Go to sleep, Juan," I said to him.

He did not like that crib, but the funny thing about him was whenever you said to him, "Night, night," he would lie down, no matter what the time of day it was. I had often laughed at how well he comprehended that phrase.

Juan stood in the crib crying to get out. When I said to him, "Night, night," he laid down. He did not stop crying, but he did lie down. Our night, night, game went on until he fell asleep. I awaked the next morning telling him how big a boy he was for sleeping in his bed. Juan normally slept with me, and I had missed his being there throughout the night.

The crib caught the doorway, and my struggle to get it loose brought me back to reality. I began to cry. I sat on the floor all alone, crying painfully about Juan and the turn my life had taken. I lay curled in a fetal position begging God to hold me. As I sobbed, I felt a peace within me and a gentle rocking of my body that held me until my crying stopped. I got up, finished Juan's room and later returned to the hospital.

Juan had grown a great deal in a short time. He literally grew before my eyes. None of his T-shirts fit anymore. My baby was growing and I could not see him reach the milestones, the way a mother would want to.

The day before Juan's release, the nurses from the company came to meet us at the hospital. The manager introduced them as her best nurses.

"This is Tammy and Alice. They both have been with our company for a long time and are two of the best nurses we have. This is Bethany. She is in training. Tammy has a lot of experience with home transport and will be the one riding with you to watch over Juan on the trip home." We shook hands and greeted each other with a smile.

"Okay, I am just ready to go home," I said.

She explained the roles the other two nurses would take in our trip home the following day. Shortly thereafter, they left.

I could hardly sleep, thinking about the next day. We were going home!

Chapter 3

After Juan spent sixty-five days in the hospital, he arrived home without incident and I settled Juan in his room. I was elated to be able to take my shoes off and just to relax on my own bed. Juan needed twenty-four hour nursing care for his first two weeks at home. As our first night home settled in, the nurse woke me up.

"Ms. Boatwright, Juan's oxygen saturation is dropping, and I don't know how to give him oxygen in line to help him maintain his levels," she said.

I jumped up and rushed in the room to assist her. I began using the ambu-bag to give him oxygen. An ambu-bag is an object used to give people with a trache oxygen. It fits over the opening of the trache and you press the body of the device which forces air into the lungs. The term used by the hospital was called, bagging. I instructed her to call 911.

I could see the level of panic on her face as she screamed. "His trache is plugged!"

I told her to calm down and that we would change the trache. I quickly removed the tube and replaced it with a new one. Juan still needed to receive oxygen.

The company that set up his ventilator failed to instruct us on how to put oxygen in line for Juan to receive. I told her to bag him as I searched for the number of the nurse from the previous shift. She had told me before she left that she would be staying the night down the street from my home, at her father's house.

I found the number and called. I told her what was going on with the oxygen. She said she was on her way. The ambulance arrived within minutes. We realized that as long as we bagged Juan, he was not in distress, but we needed to get him some oxygen.

When the previous nurse arrived, she rigged up the oxygen line so that he could get the oxygen. It was not connected the way it should have been, but it was working, and that was all that mattered.

After the paramedics and everyone left, I sat down in the chair and took a deep breath. My moment of relief was interrupted when the nurse burst out in tears.

"What's wrong?" I asked.

She sobbed, saying, "I'm sorry."

"For what? He is fine," I said.

I consoled her until she was able to regain her composure. My mother stood at the door looking confused as to why I was the one doing the consoling.

The next few days seemed to go well. There were no major problems with Juan, and I was finally able to relax a little.

I sat in the chair in Juan's room reading letters from Miss Debbie's second-grade class. I often thought of the many adults who didn't know what to say to me about Juan's situation, and those children gave me so much strength and hope.

I want to share with you a few of their letters just as they wrote them. I will write this in their grammar and using their spelling. They are seven to eight year olds.

Whitney wrote:. "This is for Juan, Please come back for Jackie. She really misses you very much and I also misses you too. I love you a lot please love me to because I have not stop prying about you. I promise I will not forget about you. Love Whitney"

The next letter read, "We hope you fill better. You are the best mom I had seened. I still pray for you at night. Jacob"

I cried, because this child could see that I was indeed trying to be a good mother to Juan, and in his little eyes I was the best.

I read on, "Dear Ms. Jackie how is Juan I hope hi is doing okay in that hospital but this is the only thing you need to remember that God is healing him as hard as he can. And God not going to give up on him as long as you keep praying. But most of all thing abot how Juan loves you and you love him. Your frind Dallas.

The last one that I will share come from Shiamante. "Dear Juan, I love you so much. I hope you get well soon! Remember God is with all of his children, don't for get I am pray for you. And I will allway rember you."

I cried as I read the hearts of those children. I could feel how hard they tried to make Juan and me feel better.

As the Thanksgiving holiday neared, my joy escalated. I knew that we would not be able to visit our family, but just knowing that we would be home for Thanksgiving made my heart feel glad.

Each day brought with it something new. I was amazed at the level of understanding that God had given me with taking care of Juan. I still look at all that I did with wonder, because I knew my level of tolerance when it came to very sick people. I had none. My stomach would always be in knots by the sight of blood, and yet here I was doing it all and not having any problems dealing with it. All that my heart knew and felt was Juan.

I spent many nights sleeping on the floor or in the chair in his room. It was very hard for me to deal with leaving him alone for quite some time. I blamed myself a lot of times for leaving him the day of his accident. I would find myself standing at his bed making promises not to ever leave him alone. It was even hard to go to the grocery store or to do other things outside of the house. Each time I tried, my fears would send me rushing to get home to him. Being into the word, I knew that God did not give us the spirit of fear. I kept repeating that God does not give me the spirit of fear until I was able to be away from him without having an anxiety attack worrying about him.

Although I knew Juan was in a coma, it looked as though he was only sleeping, and with the most peaceful look on his face. I believed in my heart that he was not suffering. As I examined his tiny little face, my mind's eye would see the face of a baby of a different race appear on his body. At first I did not understand why that happened when I looked at him, but as time passed, my heart knew the answer. What happened to Juan could have happened to any child. I had to find a way to prevent another family from going through my pain.

I could see images of the way he was in my mind and imagined his steps on the day of the accident. The innocence of a child was what my heart and soul wanted so desperately to protect.

I would often sit at his crib and talk to him. I would tell him how God was using him to help other children.

"Juan, don't be afraid. I am here, and God is there with you. It's okay to ask God to let you hold His hand. You are his special angel, and He has chosen you to fulfill His mission. It is awesome that God chose you. Just remember you have to come back to Mommy, I am here with my arms wide open, waiting for you. Today is your day for a miracle, so you get to the front of the line, my baby."

I knew he could hear me, for I could feel it deep in my bones. I would bend down to kiss him and my tears dampened his face.

"God, please give me the strength to do what I have to do to help other children not suffer through what Juan has endured."

Every day my strength became stronger.

Because of my newfound strength, I was able to sleep in my bed for the first time in a long time. I tossed and turned the first night, but it got easier to be away from him every night. I would set my alarm clock to wake we every thirty to sixty minutes to get up and check on Juan. Most of the time I woke up before the alarm went off. I thank God for watching over him for me.

One morning, I had gotten up around 3:00 to check on him. As I stood at his crib, from the corner of my eye, I saw the end of a white gown go past his door. I quickly turned, and there was no one there. I walked into the hallway and found no one there.

Thinking it was Dereck, I walked into his room to find him asleep. Then I remembered, I had prayed and asked God to place two angels at Juan's door to protect him. My fears went away. I thanked God and went to sleep.

Later, one of the nurses told me she saw the images too, but did not say anything because she did not want to frighten us. She said she too was frightened at first but had gotten used to seeing them and was no longer afraid.

With the holiday only a few days away, each day was one we truly were grateful to God for. I wished Juan could have been able to enjoy it, for it was his first Thanksgiving that he could have eaten from the table. My heart developed peace giving thanks to his being alive and home.

My mother had gone home so that she would be there for the holiday with the rest of the family. She always cooked large meals for Thanksgiving. I told her that we would be okay and to tell everyone I said hello and I wish I could have been home with them for the holiday.

Our Thanksgiving was wonderful, but the day after it that brought forth heartache.

I had gotten up early that morning to pick up supplies for Juan.

On my way past Juan's room, I stopped and asked the nurse, "Are you going to be okay by yourself with Juan? I have to go and pick up some supplies."

"Sure, Ms. Boatwright. You go right ahead; we will be fine," she responded.

I left to go to the drug store. Each step I made, my gut kept telling me that I should go home. Listening to my instincts, I jumped in my car and sped through traffic to get home.

As I rushed inside, I could hear the alarms on his machines going off. I dropped my bags at the door and ran inside his room to find the nurse just standing there looking at the machines.

"My God! Why are you not bagging him?" I screamed as I began to bag him to give him oxygen.

"I come from a nursing home background, Ms. Boatwright. There we had a DNR, and when they started to go, we let them go."

I began to pray, asking God to plant my feet. After bringing his oxygen levels up, I told her to suction his trache tube to help clear his airway.

Her sterile technique was awful. The catheter she was about to insert into his trache had touched her face, the bed, and my arm, making it no longer sterile.

As she began to insert it, I grabbed her hand to stop her. "You don't have a clue as to what you are doing, do you?" I said.

"At the nursing home we didn't have sterile technique. I told them that I was not comfortable coming out here, but they told me to just go anyway and if anything happened, to call 911," she said. I really could not understand why she did not call when it was clear that something was wrong.

I showed her the sterile process at least seven times, and she was not able to master it. It was time for his medication, so she started to draw up his medicine. I looked and was totally shocked to find the amount that she had drawn up to give him.

"What are you doing?" I asked.

"I am getting his medicine ready," she said.

"Can't you read? The bottle clearly says two point four milliliters and you have drawn up ten milliliters," I told her.

She stuttered through an excuse.

"I know you need the money for your family, so I am going to allow you to complete your shift, but you sit there in that chair until it is time for you to leave. I am going to call your office to find out why they sent you here if they knew you were not capable of taking care of Juan," I said.

She went over and sat in the chair, apologizing for her lack of knowledge. As her shift neared its end, I called her office. I spoke with the nurse who did the scheduling. I asked her why she sent her to my home knowing that she was not capable of saving my son's life.

She said. "Ms. Boatwright, I had no idea that she did not know how to do the things she needed to do."

"This woman can't bag or suction. She told me she told you all that she did not feel comfortable coming here, but you sent her anyway," I said.

"No, Ms. Boatwright, she never told us that, and she has worked with other babies on vents," she replied.

"You better stop sending her out because she is going to kill someone. Do not send her back to my home again," I said, and hung up the telephone.

My heart sank as the thought of what would have happen, had I not come home when I did. God is truly a merciful God, and I thanked Him for sending me home in time.

Later that evening, I walked into Juan's room to find his heart rate at 198 and climbing. I fell to my knees in tears. I feared that God had left me.

"God, please don't let me be put to shame for trusting in you and for waiting for you. There is something terribly wrong with my baby, and I don't know what it is. Please help me to find out," I prayed.

I got up and I began to sing *"Come by Her, Lord"*, as I picked up and straightened his room. I walked into the laundry room and came back to find his heart rate had lowered to around 140 beats. I thanked God for answering my prayer.

Later that night the next nurse came in, and I went to bed. She woke me up around 5:00 that morning.

"Ms. Boatwright, Juan's heart rate is really high. I think we should get him to the hospital," she said.

I went into his room. "How are you giving him his medications?" I asked.

"I've never given him medicine," she said.

"But here is his medical sheet that is signed after the nurses give him medicine," she explained.

I took the sheet and upon examination, found that Juan was being overdosed on three medications, two of which were very dangerous.

"Oh, my God! He is overmedicated. They have been giving him ten milliliters of Dilantin!" Dilantin is an anti-seizure medication that if overdosed, could result in death.

I called 911 and requested an ambulance. They had also given

56

him more than the prescribed amount of Potassium and Colace.

I called the nurse who did the staff scheduling.

I said, "Juan has been overmedicated by your nurses. All of you gave him ten milliliters of Dilantin, when the bottle and the doctor's orders clearly said two point four milliliters." I heard nothing but complete silence. "You are a nurse, was ten milliliters of Dilantin not a red flag to you for a child his age?"

She responded, "No."

I said, "I am asking you again, was that amount of medication for a child his age not a red flag for you?"

Again, she responded, "No."

I asked, "Do you even understand my anger?"

She responded sarcastically, "Those are your feelings. I can't tell you how to feel."

I told her that the best thing for her to do was to get me the manager on the telephone and I hung up.

As I went down the list calling each of the nurses who overmedicated Juan, they all had no explanation as to why they were giving him the overdose of medication.

While I spoke with one of the nurses, my call waiting clicked. I hung up and connected to the manager. I expressed how upset I was "You promised me that this would not happen to my baby!"

"I don't understand what could have happened. Jackie I promise you these are people I would let take care of my family," she said. The statement had become her signature line.

"Is ten milliliters of Dilantin a red flag to you for a baby Juan's age?" I asked.

"Well, that depends on the concentration," she responded.

"Where would you find the concentration of a medication?" I

asked.

She responded, "On the bottle."

"Well, if the dosage is on the bottle and they are not looking at it, I find it hard for you to convince me that they would be looking at the concentration!" I shouted.

"Jackie, I promise you these."

Interrupting her I said, "Please do not tell me that again! You have played on my religious beliefs by pretending to be a Christian. They are not taking care of your family. They are taking care of mine! You need to get me something that can justify why they gave Juan all that medicine," I said, and slammed the telephone down.

I sat in the emergency room waiting for the doctor to come in to see about Juan. Finally, he came in. I started to tell him that Juan was overmedicated.

Looking at me as though I had insulted him, he asked. "What makes you think that he is overmedicated?"

I realized that I was the one being insulted.

"Get out your calculator." I said.

He reached into his lab coat pocket and got the calculator.

"This is the doctor's orders, and this is the concentration," I said as I pointed on the bottle, showing him. "Does your calculation match the dosage on this bottle according to these orders?"

His face showed a look of intrigue. I then took out Juan's medical record sheet.

"This is what they have been giving him, with the exception of the times I gave him medicine."

"How did you learn to calculate medication dosages?" he asked.

"I learned a lot after being in ICU for such a long time," I answered.

He walked away smiling and ordered blood work on Juan. He later returned with two other doctors.

"This is the mother I was telling you about. She can calculate medicine." They all seemed shocked that a mother could learn to do something such as that.

Juan was admitted after his blood work showed his dilantin level to be .40, which is two times the safe level.

"Thank you, God," I said silently.

After Juan's Dilantin levels had lowered, we were told we would be able to go home. Dilantin is the type of medicine that leaves the body quickly once you stop giving it, but it can be very damaging at high levels when it is in the body.

The thought of going home with those incompetent nurses made me sick. I did not want to let them take care of Juan anymore. I knew that I had no choice though, because the company was the only company in Augusta that took care of children in Juan's condition.

When we arrived home, one of the nurses asked for the medical record sheet. I told her I left it at the hospital with the doctor.

"We need it back; we need to white that out," she said.

I could not believe I had heard her correctly. I did not respond, because I knew I had the medical sheet.

I didn't know how I was going to sleep, unable to trust the nurses any more. I tried, but my dreams became nightmares. I would wake up drenched in sweat and full of fear. I would race into Juan's room just to make sure that he was okay. I did not know how long I could keep this up. I could feel my body getting weary. Not from taking care of Juan but from watching them to make sure that they did nothing to cause him any further harm.

Each day I would call around trying to find another nursing company that would take Juan's case. I called the hospital social worker and asked her to help me find a new company. I expressed my feelings and how my trust in the present company had been damaged.

As Christmas approached, I was excited and grateful that my child was alive. I made Juan cassette tapes that contained Christmas songs and prayers. I started playing them for him, and he responded to hearing my voice. One of his favorite songs was the "Christmas Song."

I remember when I had taken him to have his picture taken. He was knocking over every prop the photographer put up. I started singing the "Christmas Song" and he stopped and looked at me until the song was over. We got some beautiful pictures. I would sing that same song when he got into things around the house, and he would always stop whatever he was doing and listen. The key was I had to keep singing it, to hold his attention.

The Christmas spirit filled me as I decorated the house and put up the tree. I wanted Dereck's Christmas to be a happy one. I only wished I could have gotten him all the things he wanted. He was showing a lot of courage, with all we were going through.

I sat him down and told him, "Sweetheart, Mommy is so sorry she can't get you the things you want this year, but I have been put in a difficult situation."

"It's okay, Mommy. Juan needs us right now. I understand," he said.

I grabbed him and cried. I could not believe how well he was handling things.

"Don't cry mommy. You are a good mother, and I love you," he told me.

"I love you too, baby," I said as I wiped the tears from my face.

A few days later three of my girlfriends came to visit. We all sat around and laughed about old times. They still had a way of making me laugh to the point of tears. I really needed their visit. The nurse watched Juan as we sat at my kitchen table and talked girl talk. My heart felt a little sad when I walked them to the door to say good-bye.

When I got ready for bed, I wished Juan could sleep with me. The way everything had been set up on his cart I could move it to other locations in the house. I don't think it was set up that way with the intention of moving him around, but my heart rejoiced that it was. I called Dereck in to help me. I was able to carry Juan as Dereck pulled the cart that held his ventilator.

I laid Juan on my bed. I looked at him and his eyes had opened. I praised God. Juan knew that he was in his bed. I slept close to him all night. We took him back to his room the next morning.

I got so tickled one day as I looked at the gifts under the tree. Dereck had torn a small hole in each of his gifts. I called for him to come to me. "Why did you tear holes into the presents?" I said, trying to keep a straight face.

Before he could answer, I burst out into laughter, causing him to laugh. I remembered how I did the same thing as a child, thinking my mother would never know. We both laughed. I think he needed it, too.

We began to reminisce about things Juan did.

"Mama, I bet Juan would have turned this tree over by now," he said, laughing.

"I know he would have," I responded.

"Remember how we would be watching television and it would be at the good part and all of a sudden the channel would change, and you would think I did it and I would think you did it? And it would be Juan with the remote," Dereck said.

"What about the time he hit me in the head with your drumsticks?"

I added. We continued for quite some time, going down memory lane about Juan.

Christmas was finally here, and I was glad. We opened our presents and thanked the Lord. We had our best Christmas ever, for the meaning was totally different.

The New Year would be a new beginning for us. We had somewhat adjusted to Juan's situation. I knew that deep inside, I had to do all I could to help ensure other children and their families did not go through what we were going through. The thought consumed me more and more with each passing day.

One day while attempting to balance my checkbook, I realized that I had nothing left to balance. I had given all I had to Juan's medical bills. I kept asking myself, how was I going to take care of my children? All I had was my faith that God would prepare a way for us. Although Satan tried to make me worry, something deep in me would not let me.

I'd written a brief story about Juan and all that God had done for us, and I began leaving copies at restaurants and other locations. It contained my telephone number and address.

People began to call and ask if I would pray for them. I often told God that this was too much for me, that I did not feel worthy for something of this magnitude. I allowed those who requested to come to my home, and I would pray with them.

A young girl called me and requested prayer. She told me that she was in a car accident about a year earlier. She said the doctors told her that she was fine, but she kept having headaches and dizziness. The next day she and her mother came over. I shared with her that it would be according to her faith that her healing would manifest.

We went into Juan's room and prayed. I always felt the presence of the Lord in his room. I know that she was healed. I could feel the Holy Spirit as I prayed to God for her.

How was I going to do what God was requesting me to do? I was not a perfect person, but for some reason, God had found favor in me. I remembered one of my first encounters when God spoke to me. It was about ten to twelve years ago. I was living at home. I had just finished exercising on my gym equipment I had set up in my bedroom. I was getting ready to get in the shower. As I walked toward my bathroom, I began to walk backwards, beyond my control. I was laid flat on my back on my bed, when I realized that I could not move. I was very aware of all that was happening. I heard a voice call my name repeatedly.

I refused to answer, until the voice finally said, "Jackie, this is Jesus."

"What do you want?" I asked.

"I am going to give you a business; you are going to prosper, but you will have to do something for me," the voice said.

"What is that?"

"You have to tell everybody about me."

"I can do that," I said.

"Now you can move," Jesus said.

I jumped up and ran outside to share with my mother what had happened. She told me that maybe I was dreaming. I assured her that I was not.

Now I stood in a situation where I was telling everybody about Jesus. I had been asked by several churches to tell Juan's story. God's love for him quickly spread.

Juan had an episode of elevated heart rate that required him to be back in ICU. I tried not to allow the event to break my spirits.

One day as I sat watching television in his room, I looked to find a woman standing at his door. I turned down the volume so I could hear her. She told me about her infant granddaughter who was in the room next to Juan's. She said that she was not eating and the doctors did not know why. She also said that her daughter, the mother of the baby, was torn up about all this.

She asked me if I would pray with her. I said yes.

We went to the consultation room where the young woman was. I sat down and began to share with her all that God had done for Juan. I asked her, "Are you saved?"

She replied, "No."

I told her the importance of her salvation and the healing she wanted for her baby. She nodded her head in understanding.

She asked me, "Will you pray for my baby?"

"Sure, I will," I said.

We went back to the ICU and the baby's room. We were not able to go in the room, because the doctors were trying to get an IV started on the baby. While we stood outside waiting, I told her that she must listen for the voice of God to speak to her. Quite some time passed, and the doctor still had not gotten the IV in the baby.

I told the young woman that because we could not pray for the baby at that time, she could get saved now. I led her through the scripture of salvation.

It wasn't five minutes later, when the doctor walked out into the hallway where we were standing and said, "Thank God, we finally got the IV in her."

I told the young woman that God had just spoken to her. The doctor could not even take credit for getting the IV started. We embraced, and I thanked God for doing only what I knew he could have done.

The next day the young woman and I would have several conversations about things she was going through. I shared with her similar situations that I had gone through. I warned her about Satan, and how he was going to come at her, now that she was saved. I told her she needed to be prepared to pray harder than ever before.

Juan was released from the hospital the next day. I told the woman and her mother to remember all that I shared with them and that everything was going to be all right. For some reason I felt my leaving made her apprehensive about her strength and faith in God. I reassured her of her strength and that God would not leave her alone.

When Juan and I got home, it came to me that Juan's heart rate calmed the same day the young woman was led to salvation. I often wonder if God sent us to the hospital for that very reason, the young woman and her baby.

Later that week the young woman was constantly on my mind. I called the hospital to inquire how she was doing. I could not remember the baby's name.

After being transferred to several extensions, I asked the operator to transfer me back to the ICU. Juan had been a patient there so many times that all the nurses knew me. I asked her the name of the baby who was in the room next to Juan's when he was there a few days before. She told me the name and transferred me to the fourth floor, where the child had been moved. As soon as the young woman answered the telephone, I knew that my telephone call was led by God.

"Jackie, I am so glad you called me. The doctors are saying that they may have to put her back in ICU," she said.

"You listen to me. Satan is trying to test your faith. I am going to hang this telephone up, and I want you to pray to God and rebuke him out right now. You were saved according to the word of God. I will call you back in a few minutes," I said.

About twenty or thirty minutes passed, and I called her back. Her voice this time projected a sound of true happiness.

"Is everything okay?" I asked.

"Yes, the doctor just walked in and told me that he was not sending her back to the ICU." We both praised God.

"See, I told you He is a man of His word," I said.

The baby's ailment turned out to be something simple. She started taking her formula, and the family went home.

During another episode when Juan had to go back into ICU, the little girl with cancer was brought back into the unit. After we were released from the hospital, I found out that she lost her battle. I knew that those people had great faith in God. I told myself that she was one whose life had been written with a short number of days.

My calling around for a new nursing company finally paid off. Another pediatric home nursing company had recently opened a branch office in Augusta. I called and they agreed to take Juan's case. I was not expecting any miracles, just some relief from what I was feeling toward the nurses that overmedicated Juan.

When the new company took over, I made it clear about all that I had gone through, and that I was not going to go through that again, if I could help it.

Things went okay for the first few weeks. I was shocked when one of the nurses questioned the fact that I was giving Juan cereal. I made it clear that he was my child, that he was eating pizza and chicken before his accident, and I knew that he could not survive on just formula.

"If you want to continue with my case, you better realize this is my child, and I am going to do anything I can to help him get better. He is going to be fed his cereal, and that is the bottom line," I told the case manager.

Juan soon progressed and was able to tolerate baby food from the jar through his feeding tube. After I had begun to feed him the baby food, I could tell that his strength increased. His blood work was always excellent. His doctor said that everything about a child that makes him grow was working great with Juan. I thanked God for laying on my heart and mind to feed him.

One of the nurses with the new company had a friend who was a nurse and a paramedic and she told her about Juan. She said that her friend wanted to take care of Juan. I told her sure. I felt if anybody could be an asset, a nurse who was also a paramedic would be wonderful. I considered her coming to be a blessing from God.

A few weeks passed, and I asked the nurse why I had no heard from her friend. The nurse said she did not know. Finally she came over for me to meet her. Her name was Frances. After Frances's first day of orientation, I told her she had the job.

During one of her visits, she told me that she heard the initial call when my son's accident happened. Frances asked if I wanted to know what she had heard over the radio. At first I hesitated, and then I asked that she tell me.

"Well, when the call came through and we heard it was a baby, you could hear a pin drop in our station. The paramedic at the scene was working very hard, but when I heard the drugs she had to give him, I knew he had expired," Frances said.

My heart became full, and I cried. Just imagining all that Juan went through hurt me a lot. I knew that no matter what had happened, God had brought him back to me. Hearing her recall that day hurt on one hand, but it was like medicine to my soul on the other hand.

We grew closer. Her love for Juan was evident. I would later ask her to be his godmother. One time Frances called me into Juan's room.

"Jackie, have you noticed Juan's eyes?" she said.

"What do you mean?" I responded.

"Well, when I look in his eyes, I see eyes looking back at me, but they are not his eyes. It is almost like Jesus is looking at you," she said.

"I know what you mean. I have had my experience with his eyes as well. One time I was holding him, and as our eyes met, all I could do was cry and repent," I told her.

She told me of another nurse saying something similar happened to her.

Sometimes I would start singing to Juan, and before I knew it, the Holy Spirit would fill the room, and my praises to God would be all you could hear. It was the most awesome feeling to have the spirit of God take over my body, mind, and soul.

My friends had begun to wonder about my social life, thinking that I was not taking time for me. I really had not thought about my social life. I was having a great time taking care of Juan. I was somewhat of a homebody anyway, so I was comfortable with being home.

To take you to a lighter side of this story: All of my girlfriends had the perfect man for me. My girlfriends would spend time laughing, because they were never able to match me with anyone I liked, but the time we spent trying to find Mr. Right was fun, for my joy came more from the presence of my friends than their attempts to get me hitched. I kept telling them that God would take care of that part, too.

I remember one of them saying. "Girl, God has so much to do, let us give him a little help."

Their craziness brought laughter from deep within me.

I used to tease one of my single girlfriends, "Girl, we are never going to find a man who is going to put up with our being so headstrong and outspoken."

She would always give the same answer each time. "I am not going to claim that. God is going to send me my man."

I would laugh and say, "I know he is, and you know I was just kidding."

We would always burst into laughter, and she would sum it up by saying, "Girl, you better stop saying that, before God hears you."

I truly thank God for those who stuck by me throughout my ordeal. I prayed that God would bless them for doing so.

My plight to help other children led me to the issue of liability insurance requirements for state-licensed child daycare centers. The center where Juan stayed had no liability insurance; therefore, there was no legal or financial recourse for reimbursement for the injury he sustained. I knew that other parents needed to be aware that there was no legal requirement that daycare centers have insurance, and there was a strong possibility that the daycare facility they used for their child was uninsured.

I called one of the local TV stations and asked to speak with a reporter. The secretary transferred me to a reporter. He was excited about the story, and unaware that there was no state law requiring child daycare centers to have liability insurance.

The reporter came to my home and taped the interview. During the taping, I became overwhelmed as I recalled what happened on September 9, 2001, and we had to stop the taping for me to regain my composure. Later that night I watched the interview on the local news show.

In the story, the reporter also interviewed one of our state representatives. I had previously shared with her my son's story and told her what I wanted to see done to help other children and families, who might find themselves in similar situations. The last time we talked, she shared with me that she was afraid that it would be difficult to persuade her fellow lawmakers to do anything about this issue. I could not understand why she would think that would difficult to convince the lawmakers, when we were talking about children. I never heard anything from the state representative again about the law.

As the weeks passed, I kept calling, trying to get any lawmaker I could to listen to what I was saying. This was not a local issue; it affected our state.

I called Information and requested the names and numbers for state representatives in other cities. My next call went to Savannah, Georgia. I spoke with a senator and briefly told him my story and asked if he would allow me to come to his office and meet with him. He agreed. I placed calls to the media in that area to let them know my story, and they all requested interviews on my visit to Savannah.

I knew I needed to go to Savannah, but the thought of being that far away from Juan scared me. What would I do if something happened to Juan? How would I get back home quickly enough to be with him? I had prayed to God for his safety while I took this trip. In a brief flash in my mind, I almost wished he were in the hospital so that I knew he would be where he needed to be if something happened.

The day before my trip to Savannah, June 6, the first time since Juan's accident, I went to work at my fitness center. I was having a difficult time being away from him so I called home to check on Juan. This was another day that I can only say, if it had not been for the Lord who was on our side. I share the date because of the similarities with initial accident.

The nurse answered and said, "He is doing fine. He is sitting up in his chair."

Although Juan was in what was called a semi-coma like state, he was able to sit in a specially designed chair. Sitting him up was also done for purposes of repositioning his body so that he was not in one position for long periods of time.

Within a few minutes, I heard his machines go off in the background. I knew all of those sounds too well.

"His oxygen levels are dropping; you need to bag him." I said nervously.

"Oh my God, call 911!" she screamed.

"Oh, God, please help him," I prayed.

"I don't care what you do, don't stop bagging him!" I said to her.

I attempted to dial 911 from the telephone at my business, but all I got was the local city's 911 where my business was located.

I called the sheriff's office in Augusta and told them, "My baby is on a ventilator; he is in respiratory distress. Please get an ambulance to my house now! I live at 2572 Lincolnton Parkway. Please get someone out there to help my baby," I said.

I also called Juan's nursing company and asked the case manager to call 911. I ran from the building, quickly locking the door behind me. I was forty-five minutes away from home. I turned my emergency flashers on and sped off. I was suddenly taken back to September 9.

I started calling my family members, sobbing, trying to explain as best I knew how, that something had happened to Juan. I called my home again. There was no answer. I hurt all over.

I began to kick and scream, "God please don't take my baby! You promised."

I called Frances on her cellular telephone because I knew she was

71

a paramedic and would know what was going on with Juan.

"I am in route, they are taking him to Eisenhower," she said.

"Is he alive, Frances?" She did not respond.

I screamed at the top of my lungs, releasing all of my pain and then there was a sense of peace that came over me.

"What if you have an accident and hurt yourself? Juan is in God's hands, and there is nothing you can do," I heard a voice say.

I slowed my car, and I started to talk to God in the same peace he had showered on me. I drove to Eisenhower not knowing if Juan was alive, but at peace with myself.

As I neared the military base, my telephone rang. It was Frances. "He is okay. He has a heart beat," she said. I was elated.

They sent a military police escort to lead me to the hospital emergency room. I walked in and found Juan surrounded by doctors and nurses. Many of them were there on September 9 and remembered him.

The ambulance transported Juan back to the Children's Medical Center once he was stable. My prayer was answered. It wasn't necessarily the way I would have preferred, but Juan was in the hospital when I went to Savannah. I knew that Satan was doing all that he could to stop me from making the trip. God protected us, and again reminded me that He was still protecting us.

Chapter 4

When my attorney and I arrived in Savannah, the reporter had already interviewed the senator from Savannah on the issue. My attorney and I sat down in the room. I shared my thoughts while the reporter and the senator listened attentively. "I feel safe to say the people I had come in contact with thought as I did in regard to insurance; I assumed daycare centers had to have it in order to obtain a state license."

The senator and those in the room began to tell me how courageous I was trying bring change to protect other children. I did not feel courageous; I felt like a mother. I had to do something so that Juan's injury was not in vain. I did not want what had happened to him to disappear like dust in the wind. Even more, I knew I was on a mission for God.

The senator favored my request for liability enforcement on state-licensed child daycare centers in Georgia. I interviewed with all the television stations in Savannah. I was overjoyed that somebody listened to me.

I contacted Greg, the newspaper reporter from Augusta Chronicle, and asked him to come out and allow me to share with him my desire to see a new law implemented to require state licensed daycare centers to have liability insurance. After the story ran in the paper, Greg said the story prompted several telephone calls from local citizens commending me and offering any assistance they could with what I was going through. I could not take credit for my strength; I had to give credit to God.

A few weeks later, I received a letter from the Governor Roy Barnes. I had written to him not really expecting a response. I opened the letter and was totally touched by his sincerity and the fact that he addressed Juan by name. In his letter he arranged a meeting between the commissioner who headed the Child Licensing Division and me, in Atlanta, Georgia.

Prior to my going to Atlanta, Juan celebrated his second birthday, and I thanked God for Juan's milestone. I knew that it was by the grace of God, that Juan made it to that day. We celebrated with a program and dinner at our church in Millen, the town where I grew up. Juan was provided an ambulance for the day to transport him on the fifty-mile trip.

Many of our friends and family members showed up to help us celebrate this remarkable day. I presented plaques to the firefighters and 911 personnel for their roles in saving Juan's life. I could tell that many people were amazed that Juan had lived as long as he had considering the injury he suffered. God had truly found favor in us.

My mother came and stayed with Juan while I went to Atlanta for the meeting. When I walked into the commissioner's office, he extended his hand and said, "I want you to know that I agree with you. Child daycare centers in Georgia should be insured." I felt pleased.

The licensing director for Department of Human Resources was also present. He introduced himself to me. I could tell by his responses that he was not keen on the idea of enforcing insurance on daycare centers.

"You know, the parents are not going to like the idea of the cost of daycare going up if there is enforcement of insurance," he said.

"Well, I'd like for you to ask any parent to exchange places with me for one hour," I responded.

He got quiet. For some reason, he was never able to look directly at me. The commissioner asked that he go down the list of states that do require liability insurance on state licensed daycare centers.

"I am sure you already have done a lot of research on this, Ms. Boatwright; you seem very knowledgeable on the issue," the commissioner said.

"Yes, I have and I am familiar with the fact that there are about twenty-two states that do not require liability insurance. Georgia does not need to be on that list. We need to be on the insured list," I responded.

"Sure we do," the commissioner said.

After the director finished the list, he said, "The cost for insurance is going to be very high, and some smaller daycare centers are not going to be able to afford insurance."

"If they can't afford it, sir, maybe they don't need to be in business. We are talking about children, not someone repairing your roof incorrectly or installing a plumbing fixture wrong. Millions of parents opt to use daycare every day so they can to provide a living for their families. We need to make sure the operators are accountable if a child is injured, and the only way to do that is by enforcing insurance statutes.

When I saw the state license, I automatically assumed there was insurance. Can you imagine the number of parents who are just like me? We leave our children, and we walk out of the door with the sense of security after seeing a state-issued license. The state license means so much more to a parent than someone who does not have a license. We have to protect the children," I said.

The commissioner asked, "Are you supposed to meet with some of the representatives at the capitol?"

"Yes," I responded.

"Tell them that if they need any assistance in writing the bill to let me know," he said.

I silently praised God as I thanked the commissioner for his time.

After our meeting was complete, the commissioner had his assistant drive me over to the capitol, where I met with Representative Brooks. He assured me that the bill was going to be written and on the floor of the House during the 2003 general assembly.

On my way home, I called the television stations in Augusta to share the good news. They were eagerly waiting to hear how my meeting in Atlanta turned out. I was at that moment one of the happiest women in the world. I felt I had almost won my battle.

I returned home to find Juan was doing great. I was glad that my mother was there with him. She listened to the details of my trip with as much as excitement as I had in telling her. She told me the local news aired clips of my visit several times throughout the day while I was in Atlanta.

"You know, Mom, I never told you how much it helped me when you told me to take this thing all the way on yesterday," I said.

"I know how much this means to you, and I want you to know I am proud of you," she said.

I went on to share with her about a dream I had one night, of being invited to take a tour of the "most beautiful cemetery in the world." In my dream I walked through the cemetery in awe at how beautiful it was. All the graves were those of babies. Some of the graves had twins, triplets, and even quadruplets. I remember walking out, but not much more after that.

Another dream involved seeing a baby in a casket. The face on the baby was Juan's. I awoke drenched in sweat. I ran into his room and saw that he was okay. I could not hold back my tears as I bent down, held him, and wept. A few hours later I received a telephone call. The baby that was at the end of the hall when Juan was first in the ICU had died. I hurt for the mother. I reflected on her dreams of Juan and her baby waking up at the same time. I was a bit frightened. I prayed to God to give me strength to endure the tragedy. He did.

In another dream, my telephone rang. When I answered, it was Robin. She asked how I was doing and began to talk about old times. I remember crying and thinking that she did not realize she was dead, but her laughter was joyful, and in my dream, I stopped crying and started laughing with her, because I knew she was in heaven. I do believe only heaven can bring the joy I could hear in her voice.

I had received a letter from Richard, my attorney, about the second hearing date in the case against Maria. I was very hesitant about going back to trial because during the first hearing the Judge seemed to show no compassion for my baby. The first hearing took place a few months prior to the second hearing. I filed suit against her to show the devastation a situation like mine could cause a family.

At the first hearing, a few months prior to the second hearing, before the clerk called my case in front of the judge, I sat in the court-room for more than an hour listening to an argument about a zoning map.

Maria did not even show up for court during either of the hearings.

During the first hearing after the judge called our case number, Richard attempted to apprise him of our case, but the judge began to wave his hands as though we were wasting his time.

"You don't have to go tell me all that; I can read," he said in a sarcastic tone. My stomach wrenched.

"What's the purpose of this lawsuit? What state of being is the child in?" he blurted.

As Juan's pediatrician was asked to respond, my emotions took over. I listened as the doctor told the court that Juan would be dead by the age of two years and the quality of life he would have would not be the best.

I gasped, as the contents of my stomach raced toward my throat. Tears streamed down my face as I turned to Richard. He felt my pain, and gave me his look of encouragement not to run. I sat there unable to control my silent cries until the judge dismissed the case, asking both attorneys to return with case law on timeliness of filing court motions.

I stood out in the hallway and waited for Richard to come out of the courtroom.

Maria's attorney approached me. "I am very sorry for what happened to your son, Ms. Boatwright. I am a parent, too. I just wanted you to know that."

My deepest thoughts were to slap his face; instead, my quick prayers provided me the ability to nod my head in acceptance of his remark. You see it was only moments before while inside the courtroom he talked of Juan as though his little life meant nothing.

Richard and I walked outside and stood in front of the courthouse building waiting for the television reporter to set up for an interview.

"I can't do this interview, Richard," I said to him.

"I understand; I'll take care of it," he responded.

I walked away still feeling the pain from the hearing. I saw two men carrying a cross in front of the courthouse building. I approached them and asked the meaning of what they were doing.

They began to explain that they were protesting on behalf of Christ. One of them asked, "Why are you crying?"

I shared with them Juan's story. They were familiar with it after reading the many articles from the paper. I sobbed as they prayed to God for me and for Juan for the first time I understood what it meant to carry my cross.

During the second hearing, Richard provided the judge with a copy of the case law about time limits on filing motions. The other attorney did not have a case to present to the judge.

I thought maybe the judge's demeanor would have changed, since the last time we appeared before him. I was wrong. This time God had given me the strength to look directly at him.

I guess he saw on my face the hurt he was causing me, as he began to explain, "Ms. Boatwright, I don't want you to think I have no compassion for your baby, because I do. I also want to commend you for all you are doing to get a law passed requiring daycare centers to be insured. They need to have insurance."

"Thank you," I said.

As the hearing proceeded, Richard asked if I could address the court. The judge placed me under oath and allowed me to speak.

"There is no amount of money you can give me today that would replace the life of my child or erase all he has endured. I know that you are wondering because of his condition, what is the purpose of a lawsuit. His condition should not take away from what he is legally and rightfully owed for his suffering due to the negligence of someone else.

"Juan is not brain dead. He opens his eyes. He cries real tears.

79

When he is given his baby shots at his pediatrician's office, he pulls away in pain and has to be held like normal child. He makes noises and attempts to talk. He can move his arms and legs. He also can stay off his ventilator for about two hours sometimes, breathing on his own.

"I believe in my heart he is going to get up. He is making a lot of progress. It is just going to take some time. I have a right to hold on to that hope. I pray the court will award him what he is entitled," I said with a tearful tremble in my voice.

The judge ruled the case in my favor and said he would make an award amount when he was presented with information from Juan's doctor. I told Richard that I could not assist him with getting the information, because I could not bear to hear someone put a number on Juan's life. He understood and agreed to handle it on my behalf.

As I started writing this book, God let me know that he was not through with me. I had called a friend of mine who told me a high school classmate of hers was in the hospital. He was in a four-wheeler accident and was in the ICU in a coma. She said she told the family about the young man on the fourth floor, the one I had prayed for. She also told them how the doctors had given up on him, but through prayer, he walked out of the hospital.

The Holy Spirit led me to visit her friend in the hospital. I was led by his sisters to the ICU room where he lay comatose. I read the fifth chapter of the book of James. I anointed his head and began to pray.

The minister told the family that the man could not receive salvation, because he could not respond. I believed that comatose patients could hear those around them. I told the man if he could hear me, to talk to God in his mind. I asked God to listen to his heart, because even if he could respond, with all of the tubes in his throat he wouldn't be able to do so. I began to intercede to God on his behalf. I recited the scripture of salvation.

Just as my prayer ended, the man opened his eyes. His family was in shock. Tears streamed down their faces.

"He's awake!" one of them said.

I asked him, "Did you receive the scripture of salvation?"

He nodded his head. I praised God as I shared in their excitement.

As I was about to leave, they led me down the hall to another waiting room. They introduced me to a family whose daughter had been in a bad automobile accident. The victim's sister led me to the ICU to pray for her. Their mother was at the injured girl's side, she was heavily sedated and on a ventilator due to damage to her lungs from the accident. I could feel the presence of God the moment I walked in the room.

I began to pray, and the Holy Spirit, took over, I spoke directly to God in tongues. A few later, I was told the young woman was released from the hospital to go home.

Chapter 5

Juan continued to slowly progress. The little things felt like tremendous things, in my heart. Each day brought forth eye twitches, nasal flaring, and slight movements in his lips and fingers. I am sure many may call this small, but it is when we can tell God thank you for the little things is when we can expect Him to bless us with big things.

In effort to help him progress I made several cassette tapes for Juan, encouraging him to open his eyes, get up and keep fighting to come to me. I made tapes that taught him his ABCs, his name, his body parts and even tapes that encouraged him to try to talk.

One day when Juan was about three years old, I was in the kitchen. I began to hear a noise that sounded like moaning. As I stopped to listen closely, I realized that the noise came from the back of the house. I headed down the hallway and realized the noise was coming from Juan. I had turned on a tape of me encouraging him to talk, and telling him where to place his tongue to make the sounds was working. My heart was overjoyed to see God at work.

Juan had become quite playful. He did something with his stomach that was funny. I encouraged him to pooch his tummy and he contracted his stomach muscles so that the sides of his stomach quickly contracted. I stood at his bedside laughing at each stomach thrust he made, following my request. In addition, if I asked him to move his fingers or open his eyes, he would eventually do so.

God is truly faithful to those who wait for Him. Hebrews 10:23 says, "Let us hold fast the profession of our faith without wavering: (for he is faithful that promised)" If we can learn to wait for God we will soon find that God is working.

Juan was really growing and it hurt my heart that Anthony, his father, chose not to be more active in Juan's life. Anthony would, however, call every so often and inquire how Juan was doing. One day, when Juan was around three and a half years old, I asked Anthony to come over and cut Juan's hair. I was really surprised when he came. Juan's hair had grown long and once Anthony cut it, their resemblance to one another was remarkable. I could tell from the smile on Anthony's face he felt somewhat proud that he had done something special for Juan after cutting his hair.

"Wow, that looks great!" I said to Anthony.

"When did the doctors say he was going to get off all of this equipment?" Anthony asked.

"You ought to know by now that my faith is in God, not the doctor. I told you I am no longer concerned with what the doctors think about my son. They made it perfectly clear what they thought before we left the hospital," I said. "Look, Anthony, everytime we talk, which we both know is not that often, you never have anything positive to say. Look how much he has grown and how beautiful his skin is; how pretty his teeth are. Look at how healthy he is. Does any of that matter to you?"

"There you go! I just can't stand to see him with all this stuff connected to him," he responded."

"Well, I love him just the way he is, and I am grateful to God that he is still here. If you truly love him, you would love him regardless, Anthony. That is what they call unconditional love!" I said, walking out of the room.

I could hear Anthony collecting his things as I sat in the living room on the couch asking God to help me through confrontation.

Anthony entered the living room. Our eyes met, and he knew I was upset. I only wished that his faith was where my faith was. He walked past me to exit the side door. I thanked God that Anthony was gone. I was glad that he had made the effort to do something for his son, but after further thought, I soon began to see that Satan had actually found a way to try to get me to lose my faith in Christ.

I sat there hurting for Juan, praying that God continue to give me the strength to stand on my faith in Him. I began to reminisce about a day when Juan was much younger and I was carrying him in his carrier seat into an office building. As we were walking up the sidewalk toward the entrance, a man and a woman were coming out of the door.

"Where is the father of that baby?" the man asked.

"Excuse me?" I asked. Who was this man and why was he asking me where the father of my child was, I thought. Unknown to me, I began to explain what had happened between Anthony and me to the man, a complete stranger.

"Well, he has been gone since I was two months pregnant, and he got married when I was eight months pregnant," I said.

The next words that came from the man sent chills throughout me but, I really did not know why at that time.

"Woe to that man! He is going to wish he rather had a millstone tied around his neck and cast into the sea, for what he has done to this child," he said as he pointed to a wide-eyed Juan in the baby carrier.

I stood like a statue, unable to move or speak for a brief moment. That day would be further explained a few years later.

Hearing the alarms on Juan's machine brought me back to the present. I got up to check on him. I kissed him softly on his cheek as he lay there with his new haircut. I wondered why the incident with the strange man was brought back to my memory nearly three years later.

I was overjoyed when I finally got a senator to introduce my bill to the Senate Committee on Children and Youth. His name was Senator Don

Cheeks, an older white male with a very strong southern accent. I was truly grateful to him because it finally appeared that things were beginning to happen. I had presented the senator with all of my research on the proposed bill, including its language.

The bill did not enforce insurance; instead it required day care centers to post the fact that they were uninsured as well as tell the parents and get in writing that the parents were aware that they were an uninsured child daycare center. I felt strongly that this stipulation would be the best route to ensure that Georgia made an effort to protect the most fragile of its citizens.

I would find out a few weeks later through a telephone call that the chairwoman of the committee wanted to know if I would be interested in speaking before the committee concerning the proposed bill. I was elated to do so. The chairwoman's secretary gave me all of the particulars for the hearing.

A few days before I had to go to the capitol, I was once again in child support court with Anthony. I could not understand why it was so hard for him to see the need to take care of Juan, especially knowing what I was facing.

As usual Cheryl showed up to court. She was shocked when the bailiff told her the issue had nothing to do with her, and she could not come into the courtroom.

I had been told that the judge really cared for children and he was hard on parents who did not take care of their children. Needless to say, we would go in only to find out that he was not the judge who was to hear our case. He sternly balked at Anthony for being late and quickly adjourned the case after suggesting that I contact the child support recovery unit to assist me with collecting child support from Anthony.

He and Cheryl walked out on that day all smiles, especially because it was their wedding anniversary. I prayed that God would bless them ,and I knew in my heart that God would take care of Juan.

I arrived at the Capitol in Atlanta with my prepared speech. I sat in a room full of people, all who has some cause or issue that affected children in some capacity. There was a large conference table in the center of the room, and around it sat the committee chairwoman and the committee members. All of these people were also state legislators. The people like me who were there to address the committee sat in chairs that were lined against the wall around the entire room. I was surprised to see the new governor's wife. She was there to speak on the importance of foster parents for abused and neglected children. She was a very petite woman, but her message was very strong. Also present to my surprise was the judge who was in charge of the child support court I had filed against Anthony a few days before.

When my name was called to speak, my heart fluttered, but I knew that I had to speak up for the other children who might find themselves in Juan's position. I stood poised and walked gracefully to the end of the conference table and read my speech, which I hoped would persuade the committee to send my bill to the Senate floor for vote.

> I am here today on behalf of my son, Juan, and the many children who are in child daycare facilities in the state of Georgia. On September 9, 2001, my son fell into a bucket of mop water at his state-licensed, child daycare center. He is currently at home on life support.

> I had no idea that the center was uninsured and was never informed of that fact during the entire time my son was left there. Now I stand here before you emotionally, mentally, and financially devastated and without any re- course for the state-licensed center that had no liability

insurance or no legal obligation to inform me that there was no insurance.

The state of Georgia takes pride in protecting our children. If we are indeed going to do so, then we must start with this law, Senate Bill Twenty-Four. This great oversight, if not corrected or regulated in some form, is going to produce more situations like mine, when a parent or parents are torn between their parental obligations to an injured child and trying to maintain the basic necessities, such as food, clothing, and shelter.

The state-issued license gave me a sense of security that if our state endorsed an individual to care for children, then the endorsed individual was a cut above someone who did not have a state license. I was not given the opportunity to exercise my freedom of choice, because I was not informed of a very important fact that could have very well changed my life as it is today. We have to provide ways to give recourse to parents and to hold accountable in the event of negligence those individuals who are licensed by the state as child daycare operators in any capacity.

It is becoming more frequent that children are subjected to negligence at daycare facilities in our state. If our state is not going to enforce insurance, please do the next best thing, enforce disclosure. Make daycare operators tell the parents, and let the parents make the decision. If my son's life meant anything, it would be that no family has to go through such a tragedy, and on top of the tragedy struggle from day to day to make ends meet while the individual whose negligence caused the turmoil is left unaccountable and is able to move forward in life.

Just as that state license was disclosed to me, whether the center was insured or not should have also been disclosed to me. Instead, I was not informed, and because of the assumption of state requirement after seeing a state license, as it is assumed by the many parents that I have come in contact with, I left my child with an uninsured, state-licensed child daycare facility.

This law is essential for reasons of economic security, peace of mind, and public relations. I am living proof of the costs when adverse events occur at a child daycare facility and how it can easily cause a financial disaster that can disrupt the care of children as well as destroy the livelihood of families. Please, in honor of my son Juan, and to protect other children and families, pass Senate Bill Twenty-Four.

I ended my speech. My eyes had become full of tears, and I could hear nothing but complete silence in the room.

One of the senators broke the silence. "How in the world can anybody in their right mind open a daycare center and not have insurance? That is the most ridiculous thing I have ever heard. It is insane," she said, looking around the table at her colleagues.

"I am going to have to decline to vote on this issue simply because I work at a daycare, and there may be some conflict of interest," she went on to say.

"How do you all vote on the proposed legislation?" the chairwoman asked the committee members.

They all voted unanimously to send Senate Bill Twenty-Four to the

Senate floor for a vote to become law. I was equally shocked when the judge sitting next to the senator whispered in his ear. I am not sure what he said to him, but right afterwards, the senator stood and made the motion for the bill to be named in honor of my son. The motion was accepted that Senate Bill Twenty-Four be named Juan's Law.

I left the room with my heart so full I thought it would burst out of my chest. I could hardly wait to share the news with my family. I arrived home to newspaper and television interviews about my trip to the Capitol. I kissed Juan and Dereck.

"Mom, I am so proud of you." Dereck said.

I embraced him and told him how much I appreciated him for being such a big boy throughout this ordeal. Dereck was truly instrumental in my strength. He assisted many nights when Juan got unstable when I first brought Juan home. He had become a teenager and was growing like a weed. He was as tall as me.

When I was pregnant with Juan and the doctor put me on bed rest because of a previous miscarriage, I was considered high risk. Dereck knew that I could not get out of bed, so he refused to go outside and play. He was determined to take care of me. I heard the door bell ring and he answered it.

"No, I can't come outside to play, I have to take care of my mom; she is sick." he would say.

His refusal to go outside because I was on bed rest, went on for about three days, when I finally told him that I would be okay, and he could go outside to play with his friends.

"Who is going to watch you?" he asked.

"I will be fine, little boy," I responded

I had been teaching Dereck how to do many things. He knew how to vacuum, and I had been letting him cook certain foods.

"I will go, out but I will cook you some French fries before I go, okay, Mommy." He said.

"Okay, sweetie. Remember what Mommy told you about the stove," I responded.

I could smell those French fries, and I really was hungry. I had been suffering with severe nausea throughout the majority of my pregnancy, so I really needed a break from the ginger ale and saltine crackers I had been eating for a few days.

As I lay there in anticipation of the delicious smell from the French fries, I could hear Dereck in the background.

"Here I come, Mommy!" he yelled out.

When he finally reached the bedroom, he had the largest plate of half-cooked French fries I had ever seen.

"Oh, honey, these look great!" I said, wanting him to know that I appreciated him for making me something to eat.

I knew that there was no way that those French fries were going to stay on my stomach. Waiting for him to leave the room seemed like eternity.

After his speech telling me to stay me in bed and get rest, he headed for the bedroom door. He reached the door way and turned with a very serious look on his face. "Mommy, whose French fries are the best, mine or McDonald's?"

I had to think quickly, because I knew that he was the only cook in the house at the time, plus a few minutes in the microwave would finish cooking the fries that were on my plate. I thought for second, being careful not to think too long. "Boy, you know your fries are better than McDonald's!" I said with a smile and a wink.

"Yes!" he said and he ran down the hallway.

I lay there laughing to myself about what had just occurred.

Time had passed and he was still taking care of his little brother, but in a very different way. I would often watch him from the monitor in my bedroom, kissing Juan all over his face. I constantly encouraged him to go outside and play and never required him to take care of Juan unless I was in a situation where I needed an extra pair of hands. It was my desire for Dereck to have as normal of life as our situation would allow him to have.

After so much spiritually had happened to me I soon realized and finally heeded to my calling from the Lord. I accepted the call to ministry and was licensed. I knew that God had chosen my family and me for a very special mission, and my obedience was going to be the key to Juan's healing.

I was asked often to speak at churches near and far, to share Juan's testimony. I created a Web site for Juan, and it began to attract people from all over the world. People started sending e-mails that they were in spiritual agreement with me about Juan's healing, and they thanked me for encouraging their faith in Christ.

About a year after Juan's accident, I took him (Juan) to Hilton Head South Carolina, his first major trip from home. We had trusted God this far, so we knew that he would not leave us now.

Frances, Juan's nurse and godmother, agreed to go with us to take care of Juan during our stay. She and I decided to take Juan out to the mall. The event turned out to be like taking a major celebrity to the mall. A crowd soon gathered at Juan's feet as they listened attentively to me describing his ordeal in detail. About an hour or so later we, broke away to leave for our hotel. I shared with the nurse that I wanted purchase a disposable camera to take some pictures, because I forgot to bring mine from home.

Frances went outside the main entrance of the mall to wait for us. I

91

pushed Juan into Ritz Camera. There were only two people other than Juan and me, a young white man who was working behind the counter, and from their conversation, a black male friend who had dropped in to chat with him.

As I searched the store for an affordable disposable camera, the young white man behind the counter called out to me. It startled me, because when I entered the store they were on the opposite end of the counter.

"Ma'am, what is his name?" he asked.

Not sure to whom he was referring, I looked around to see if someone else had come into the store.

He pointed to Juan.

"Oh, I am sorry; his name is Juan," I said.

"What happened to him?" he asked

I began to share Juan's story, but when I reached the point of the doctors telling me that Juan was brain dead and going to be a vegetable, he stopped me.

"No, ma'am; he is very much alive! The moment he walked in my door, I got a glimpse of heaven."

I noticed he said *walked* into his door. I wondered what was going on, in awe at the spiritual bonding that was going on between him and Juan. Before I left store, I gave him Juan's Web page address so that he could keep up with him.

A few days after we returned to Georgia I received an e-mail from him, but it was not addressed to me, it was addressed to Juan. This is what it said:

> Dear Anthony DeJuan,
>
> I hope you remember me. You met me at the Mall at
> Shelter Cove (Ritz Camera) in Hilton Head Island, SC,
> about two weeks ago. I have been thinking about you

92

since I met you and wanted to see how your progress is going. I am very impressed with your Web site and have made it my home page, so when I connect to the Internet you are the first thing I see. The Lord has worked miracles with you and with me since our meeting each other.

My name is Brandon T. Link. I am married (Mary Martha Link) and have just recently five months ago had a baby boy named Jensen Trauger Link, I have lived in Hilton Head Island for approximately five years and worked at Ritz Camera for four years. My wife and I originally are from the great state of Oklahoma. Go Sooners! Jensen, the love of my life, was born June 17, 2002, and he has blessed me just as you, my friend, have blessed everyone you meet.

The Spirit of the Lord was laid upon you so that others might see the true love and grace of our Savior Jesus Christ. It is people like you who will draw and attract other believers and non believers to you. They will want to know "What is it about this person that makes me feel good?" You will change many lives, and it is my guess you have already, your family, your mother, your friends and me... You changed my life! I thank you for that my prayers will be with you. I do hope the Lord will bring us together again in His own time.

God Bless you and the ones around you who have allowed the Spirit of God to manifest in your heart. I appreciate your sharing just a glimpse of Heaven when you came into the store.

Your Brother in Christ Jesus

I can only imagine what the Lord had done to have such an effect as Juan so obviously had on this young man. For all that God was doing, I was grateful that he thought enough of Juan and of me to do it, through. I often said that for the many souls that have been led to Christ since this tragedy, it makes it worth it. Reading this e-mail sent chills throughout my body.

I soon learned of more good news about the law. The Senate had set a date on which the bill would come up for a vote. I traveled to Atlanta and was allowed to sit in the visitor's gallery as Senate Bill Twenty-Four was announced for a vote. As the bells in the Senate Chambers chimed, I looked at the board that monitored each vote. Senate Bill Twenty-Four passed with a unanimous vote.

I knew then that my battle was halfway won. I cannot tell you in words what that moment meant to me and to the senseless injury that Juan was suffering. I can tell you that the thought of another mother, along with the suffering of another child, facing what I was fighting was a major driving force. Senate Bill 24 had no benefits for me or for my son, but what it would do for others would give purpose to Juan's injury.

The bill left the Senate and was sent over to the House of Representatives for consideration. I was told I would be given the date when it the House would be voting on the bill.

Although I knew God truly was still with us, Satan had not given up on trying to, shake my faith. One day I came home and was greeted by the nurse.

"Ms. Boatwright, Kathy, the nursing supervisor, said we can no longer feed Juan baby food," she told me.

"What are you talking about? He has been eating baby food since the time he came home and prior to my hiring her company," I said.

I called the office and asked to speak to the nursing supervisor. "Why are the nurses are not to feed Juan baby food anymore?" I asked her.

"His doctor said that she was not going to sign off on the paperwork for Juan to be fed baby food any more, and if the doctor doesn't sign it my nurses are not going to give it to him," she responded.

"Kathy, my baby has been eating baby food since the day he came home. The hospital feeds him baby food whenever he has to stay. He is growing and thriving, and I am not going to stop feeding my child, unless you can show me some proof where feeding baby food is causing him harm. By the way to what doctor are you referring?" I asked

"His lung doctor; she said that Juan could aspirate the baby food," she responded.

"Why in the world would you take Juan's nutritional concerns to his lung doctor? You should have taken that concern to his primary pediatrician, Dr. Getts. He could aspirate anything that is given to him to eat. Dr. Hudson has never monitored Juan's nutrition or his growth. We have never had any conversation regarding what Juan should or should not eat, so why in the world would you even inquire about that with her?" I could feel that I was getting angry.

The nursing agency not wanting to feed Juan was really a true shock, because with each hospital visit, I was asked what Juan ate at home, and that was what was prepared for him to eat when he had extended stays at the hospital. You see, Satan will try every way that he can to tear you down and get you in a fix where, if you are not careful, your thoughts will be far from Christ and on matters that are there to keep you despondent, confused, and angry. Juan was growing and the food was making him stronger and healthier, and the enemy could not stand it.

I hung up the telephone and called my son's primary pediatrician office. The nurse was in total disbelief that the nursing company had taken this position.

"We have not seen any harm that feeding Juan baby food has caused him Ms. Boatwright. I am faxing an order from the doctor for the nurses to continue feeding Juan baby food," she said.

I received the doctor's order by fax shortly after hanging up with him. I took into the room and gave it to the nurse. I called the nursing supervisor back and told her what his primary doctor had said and that there was a doctor's order to continue feeding Juan baby food.

"He is not the doctor that signs the paperwork for us to get paid, so my nurses are no longer going to feed him," she responded.

"Well I am relieving your company from the care of my child. If you refuse to feed him then you can pick up your paperwork. Your services are no longer needed." I said.

The enemy had taken control of this woman. I felt for Kathy because she was battling breast cancer, and the majority of her hair was falling out. Yet she had found the strength, better yet, Satan found her weakness. Now here she was in the midst of trying to stop me from feeding my child when she knew that his being fed was helping him.

After the nurse at my home left, I took over the care of Juan. I began to cry out to God to help me and to give me the strength. About an hour after firing the company, my doorbell rang. It was a representative from the Department of Family and Children Services. She was a young black woman, very petite, who appeared to be no more than twenty.

"Ms. Boatwright, I am here to investigate a complaint about your endangering the life of your child," the young woman said.

My heart sank as tears welled in my eyes. The DFACS worker would not confirm it, yet I knew that Kathy, the nursing supervisor, had gotten angry, called DFACS, and made a false statement against me.

"We received a call stating that you submerged your child in water, you are taking him off of the ventilator, and that you are feeding him baby food, when you are not supposed to," she said.

"There is some truth to all of those allegations. Yes, I baptized my son! I am a minister and that is my religious right. Yes, I take him off the ventilator! If I don't remove him and allow him to take any breaths, how will he ever learn to breathe again? I don't want my baby connected to these machines for the rest of his life. And yes, I feed my child! I am the last person who would try to take my son's life. As hard as I have fought to keep him alive, to do that would make no sense," I said.

I tearfully explained what had happened and showed her a copy of the doctor's order for the nurse to continue feeding Juan his baby food, making note of the date and time of the fax to show her that the call, to DFACS was placed out of malice.

"Ms. Boatwright, I can look at this child and tell that he is being well taken care of. It is a formality that I have to investigate this, because a complaint was filed. But I will do my best to make sure it is over as soon as I can. I want you to know that I think you are doing a great job, and I am sure that it would be the same thing my mother would do for me, had such a thing happened to me." She said with sincere concern.

"Thank you," I said.

I signed the paperwork and she left. I fell to floor crying out to God to protect my family and me from the enemy.

Let me share with you how I made the decision to baptize Juan. One night while I was holding him, I heard the Holy Spirit tell me that I needed to baptize Juan. I sat in shock at what the Lord was asking me to do.

"Lord, if this is what you would have me do, please give me some confirmation. Keep this heavy on my mind tomorrow, and guide me through." I said.

The next morning came, and I had not heard from the Lord. Later that evening He spoke to me and told me now was the time. The request was

97

so heavy that I had to do it. I told the two nurses, who were caring for Juan on that day, that I was getting ready to baptize Juan. The strangest thing was they did not question me at all. I began to follow the instructions that the Lord was giving me as the bathtub was being filled with water.

The Lord instructed me to make a covering like a vest from plastic bags to go around Juan. It would serve as protection for his trache. The Lord reminded me of the location of swimming goggles and ear plugs that I had not touched for more than five years when I took my fifteen minutes of swimming lessons. That is another whole story.

The two nurses help me get Juan into the bathroom. I sat on the tub, holding him while I recited the baptism prayer. I sat Juan in the tub placing my hand over his nose and mouth, took him under the water, and brought him up. It was a beautiful experience, because I knew that coming up from the water represented the resurrection of Christ.

The nurses and I were in tears as Juan's body was totally relaxed after he was baptized.

I had to trust God, for it was He who told me what to tell the doctors to do to Juan when they were telling me they had done all that they could. I knew without a doubt that God was on our side and that he was going to continue to lead me in the right direction as long as I kept my eyes on Him.

I called the board of nursing to make a complaint against the nurse for not following the doctor's order to feed Juan. When you belong to God, people have to be very careful how they treat you, for God will not allow anyone to interrupt his plan, and trust me, he had a plan for us. The DFACS case was closed, and the nurse was later fired. I am not sure if it was because our situation but God has a way of letting you know that the battle is not yours, and He is ready to fight for you.

I am humbled that God gave me another opportunity to be a mother to Juan. One time I was at the track walking, when a woman began to walk alongside me. Recognizing me from the many television and newspaper interviews, she started a conversation by praising me for my efforts. Her conversation soon changed to Juan.

"It must be very hard taking care of your son in his condition," she asked.

Don't get me wrong; I don't look for negativity in everyone I meet, but I do look for the quickness of the enemy to shake my emotions. I quickly assessed that this moment could be one of those when Satan could be trying to remind me of the tedious battle I was fighting, so I prepared myself for another one of his smooth moves.

"Actually, it is the greatest blessing God could have given me. I am just so happy to have the opportunity to change another diaper and to take care of him, that his condition does not matter to me. I know in my heart this is only temporary, if I keep my faith in Christ," I told her.

"I understand now," she said as tears streamed her face.

My heart began to feel for her as we both stopped walking, so she could regain her composure.

"I lost a child in a car accident, and if I had a chance to have him back, I would take him in any condition that God gave him to me," she tearfully added.

This was not the first time someone assumed that taking care of Juan was a burden to me. Yes, we were somewhat limited in our ability to get up and go, but thank God we could go. It just took us a little longer. Having my son with me is worth everything to me; that is just how much I love him.

I will tell anyone that standing on faith is God is not an easy task, but without faith, the book of James says you need not ask God for anything and expect to receive. Being a Christian does not relieve us of trials and tribulations. You will fall down, but when you can find the courage to get up, it demonstrates your faith in God.

I walked into Juan's room every day in anticipation of him being able to do something that he was not able to do the day before. James Chapter Two, Verse eighteen says *"Faith without works is dead."*

When God asked Noah to build the ark because it was going to rain Noah did so although it had never rained before. His building of the ark demonstrated his works. Despite the fact that it had never rained, Noah built the ark because he trusted God.

We must trust God with our actions as well as our words. You must really know and believe without any doubt that God is capable of bringing you through any situation. I forever remind God of His word and His promise to completely heal Juan

Just as Satan attempted to let me know he was still trying, God reassured me that He was still there to protect me. One night during a time when my mother was visiting, my doorbell rang and a man had come to repossess my car. I knew that things were getting hard to control, but my heart and my mind knew that God would take care of our needs.

For some reason, it did not bother me one way or the other. When you have done your very best and you know that God is with you, things just don't bother you the way they would if you were not in Christ.

My mother was very worried about how I was going to get Juan back and forth to his doctor's appointments. "What are you going to do, Jackie?" she asked.

"Mom, Jackie has done her very best, and God knows that Juan has to be taken back and forth to the doctor. For some reason I am not worried. I am going to bed. I suggest you do the same." I told her as I kissed her on the cheek.

When God gives you something, no one can take it away from you, no matter how hard they try. A few days later, I received a telephone call from the finance company telling me I could come and get my car and that the finance company had lowered my monthly payments.

My friends still to this day are amazed at how God worked that situation out. I often say as you wait on God to move, you must do it not only with the utmost confidence, but also in silence, trusting Him to do what is best for you and your situation.

Our life had taken so many twists and turns but through the grace of God we managed to stand through the trials and tribulations. I had no idea that there was yet more to come in all that we have endured.

As our days turned to weeks and our weeks to months we soon realized we had spent more than three years into our struggle. There were many times when I felt somewhat like Job, sometimes like Paul and other times like Moses. I did not to know what to expect from one day to the next.

Chapter 6

Many people said that I bashed nurses by my sharing what Juan had gone through. I share those experiences because I want you to understand that the enemy will come in many forms and will use whoever is available to get to those who are standing in the name of Jesus. I have no ill feelings toward any of these people. It is Satan I have the problem with. I thank God for never leaving me to fight any of those battles alone.

One day I left Juan with his nurse. My intentions were to pick up his supplies and go to the park and do some reading; however, I became overwhelmed by a discerning spirit that I should go home instead.

I stopped at the mailbox and pulled into my driveway. I was sitting and looking through my mail when my cell phone rang. I was hesitant to answer, because I did not recognize the number on the display pad. My instincts led me to answer. "Hello." I said.

"Jackie, this is the Betty, the nurse caring for Juan. I was calling you to let you know that I was giving Juan his bath and everything just dropped," she said calmly.

"Dropped? What do you mean? Is he okay?" My heart began to pound.

"Oh yes, he is fine," she responded.

"Okay, I am in the driveway I will be inside in a moment."

It did not come to mind why the nurse was calling from the unknown number, as opposed to my home number, but when I opened my door, I soon found out why.

All of Juan's alarms were going off. I dropped the bags and raced to his room.

"Oh my God! Zero!" I screamed as I looked at the oxygen monitor. I quickly grabbed the ambu bag and to give him oxygen. As I bagged him, he would take a breath and turn from gray to blue. The reason the nurse did not call me from my home telephone was because during the entire time she told me everything was okay, she was on my home telephone with 911. The nurse was not doing anything to save Juan. While I was doing all I could, she stood in Juan's room watching me, as I frantically tried to save his life.

Each time Juan's color changed, I screamed at the top of my lungs in horror. It was the first time I actually looked in the face of death. I prayed for God to help me.

"Come on, Juan, my baby!" I said as I continued to press on the ambu bag.

"Please, God help me," I prayed.

A voice inside of me said, "Change out his trache tube."

"Get me another trache tube!" I shouted to the nurse.

"I've already changed his trache," she responded.

"Get me another trache tube right now!" I yelled.

"Calm down Ms. Boatwright." she said as though Juan was not in any danger.

As I began to undo the ties around his neck hold the trache tube in place, I realized that they were not secured, and that the trache tube was not in the stoma in his throat.

"Oh, my God! The trache is not in," I said and I quickly reinserted it.

Upon putting the trache back in, my bagging efforts worked. Juan's oxygen level returned to one hundred percent. I was exhausted by the time the paramedics arrived. Unable to move my hands from the trache tube in Juan's throat, I stood motionless as tears screamed down my face, yet my heart and lips praised God for what He had done.

Many people fail to forget I was not a nurse prior to Juan's accident and neither had I had any nursing experience, but when God calls you to a mission, he will endow you with what you need to fight your battle. Had God not sent me home when He did, Juan would not have lived. God prepared Juan for this situation months before it happened, because I had been taking him off of the ventilator and allowing him to take breaths on his own, and because God was with Juan and he had been coming off periodically, he was able to sustain himself until I got there to help him.

God truly sits high and looks low. He knows what is going to happen to us before it happens. I am truly grateful for His presence in my home and in my life.

When the paramedics arrived, I was so fixated on Juan that one of the medics had to literally pry my hands from him to assess him. I weakly walked into the hallway where I collapsed to the floor. I was helped to my nearby couch by one of the paramedics.

"It is okay, Jackie," he said.

"Thank you, Jesus," I whispered.

"Jackie, you did good. You saved him," he said.

"No, God saved him," I said tearfully.

"I know you must be going through a lot, but you are doing a wonderful job with Juan," he said as he allowed me to rest my head on his shoulder.

"Thank you," I responded.

The paramedic who was assessing Juan came out and told me that he was okay and had stabilized. I made the decision not to take him to the hospital.

When the paramedics left, I went into Juan's room to talk to the nurse to find out what happened. "Why did you change Juan's trache, when there was no need to do so?" I asked.

"I have changed a trache before, but I have never seen all of that stuff there." She used her hands to demonstrate the ties that fastened around his neck to hold the trache tube in the stoma.

The day was a very trying day for me, but it also made me see that God truly had found favor in Juan, and no matter how much the enemy tried to take him, God let me know that He was going to keep His promise and protect Juan as long as I kept my faith and my eyes on him.

On another occasion, a nurse was sent by the agency to care for Juan. I was told that she had an excellent work history and was highly recommended.

I must share with you the anointing that was upon Juan's room. God had built a hedge of protection around him and many who came to us claiming that God sent them there to take care of Juan were quickly exposed by God.

Another nurse was sent out by the agency; they highly recommended her. When I opened my door to let her in, she told me that God had sent her to take care of Juan. God soon exposed that lie.

One day after, a few weeks of uneasiness, she broke down and told me that she had recently been declared mentally insane by a judge and lost her children as a result. She stated that if the judge saw her taking care of a child like Juan she could get her children back. She went on to tell me that thirty-one people died under her care while she was charge nurse on a previous job.

Clearly this woman was in no condition to take care of Juan. I did not know this information prior to her telling me, but God has a way of bringing the darkness to the light.

I praised God as I shared with her my concerns about her taking care of my son. God continued to direct my path when it came to Juan and I am truly humbled for this kind of favor.

God will always let you know that He is still with you. Sometimes as Christians we spend so much time looking for the big blessings that we overlook the many small blessings that God gives us.

Juan had begun to have minor movement in his lips, and his eye pupils often moved from side to side. There were so many days when Dereck and I would stand there in awe at the many little miracles that God was doing for Juan.

Dereck is another blessing and a miracle as well. He had been a true champ about our whole ordeal. He was a great source of my strength and I am thankful for him. He and Juan always had a wonderful relationship. Dereck could say anything to Juan, and he would burst into laughter. My mind's eye would always remind me of them riding in the back of the car before Juan's accident.

Dereck would often lead us in prayer as we touched and agreed many nights in Juan's room. The Bible says that if any two touch and agree in prayer that what they are asking should be granted by God. I am glad Dereck knows God and how to pray, for I teach him constantly. He has always been quiet in demeanor and in spirit. I led him to salvation when he was about nine years old. When he was later baptized in the church he really took it seriously. He thought that if he missed one Sunday at church he would not be allowed to come back. As he had gotten older, neither his demeanor nor his spirit has changed.

Many nights Dereck was right there to help me when I had to rush into Juan's room. God is good, and I am blessed.

I often think of Jesus and how he suffered so that many would be saved. I think of Juan and how he suffered so that other children may be saved. I am not by any means equating Juan to Jesus, but Romans Chapter Five verse three says *"Suffering brings patience, and patience brings character, and character brings hope."*

My hope was in Christ Jesus and all that he promised to us in His word. I often thought of all the things we wait for with anticipation, when it comes to waiting for God we give up very soon. I have heard of people claiming to play the same lottery numbers for years so, why can't we wait for God to come in our times of trouble?

If I had to advise people who had to face a similar situation, I would clearly tell them to not lean on their own understanding. They will never be able to truly comprehend their troubles. Just know that God can work it out. Many asked, "Where was God when your baby was going toward that water?" He was there hurting for my son just like He was when His own son suffered needlessly at the hands of others.

We must learn to forgive and open our hearts, because anger only hurts the one who is angry. I could have spent my time hating Maria and her family, but they moved on quickly. She never once called and inquired as to how Juan was doing. God is the one and only judge, and He will vindicate your situation. I know that someday she has a higher power to answer to, and that is a day that will surely come.

Our comfort was in the word of God, knowing that the scriptures came from him to help us face tomorrow. It would have been much easier to give up, but I often thought if Christ had given up when he was carrying the cross, where would we be today?

God is very real and each and every day for us and for Juan was a testament that God is a protector.

When you give yourself completely to God, you allow him to fight your battles just as He did for the Israelites, but you have to trust Him with your troubles, and know that He is God all by himself and that He needs no help to do what He wants to do for you.

When Juan was in the hospital listening to those around me who were saying there is not way possible, God was standing there with his arms wide open, reminding me that with Him all things are possible.

I knew that God loved my son and me just as He loves you, and I can assure you that when we hurt, He hurts. Many times I have been down on my knees being deeply troubled, and just when I thought I could bear no more, God sent a ray of light and lifted the load, just as He sent the man to help Jesus carry the cross to Calvary.

Juan taught me the true meaning of suffering and patience. Each and every day I saw him take his ordeal like a little man. Every day he made significant improvement. I was proud of him, for he was standing in more of a position to give up than me, but he was indeed a fighter, and I praise God for instilling that quality in him.

I spent many days and nights standing at his bedside, kissing him all over his face. I knew that he was in there and that he wanted me as much as I wanted him. He had begun to interact with me during our play times. He would thrust his little body producing, a grunt with each one, to show me that he was hearing me talk to him.

Ever since the lead doctor labeled Juan as brain dead and a vegetable, I believed that his treating doctors looked at everything new thing he did as some type of reaction to his near drowning. If he moved his body, they called it a spasm, if he made noises, they'd say he had a leak around his trache tube. They would not even acknowledge his opening his eyes as a sign of improvement. Instead, the doctors only reminded me of whatever negative they could find.

When you know who holds your future, you will be able to place such negativity in the back of your mind. Trust God and keep him in your heart and on your mind.

I had been telling one of Juan's doctors that Juan was able to stay off the ventilator at times, breathing on his own. To them this was another impossible situation. Juan limited his activity level when we were at the doctor's office. He showed us more activity at home.

My mother came to visit us. She and I had gone shopping when the nurse caring for Juan, called me on my cell phone asking me to come home.

"Jackie the baby's oxygen levels keep dropping. I have called 911, and the paramedics are on the way," she said.

"Is he okay?" I asked.

"Yes, he is at one hundred percent, but right now I have the oxygen turned up to eight liters. I think you need to come home," she said.

"I am on my way there now." I replied.

Before we could make it home, I received another call from one of the paramedics who had become a regular with Juan. "Hello Jackie, this is Gary, the paramedic. We are here at your house with Juan. He appears fine, but what do we need to do?" He asked.

I was somewhat surprised that he had taken notice to my knowledge of Juan's care and wanted to know what I thought should be done. "Hi, Gary. If he is stable, I 'll be there in a few minutes.".

When I walked into Juan's room, I found him surrounded by paramedics and firemen. They stepped back and allowed me to assess the situation so that I could give my thoughts about what was happening.

"I think he is breathing against the ventilator," I told Gary as the alarms continued to ring.

Juan would stabilize, and then the alarms would go off again.

"Maybe we should take him to the hospital just to be on the safe side," Gary told me.

I agreed and watched as they loaded Juan onto the stretcher. The paramedics had disconnected him from the ventilator.

"I think we will bag him all the way to the hospital," One of the paramedics said.

I went to the door and told them that they were going to need his ventilator when they got to the hospital. I unplugged it and carried it outside to the ambulance. I sat it on the floor of the ambulance as Gary continued to bag Juan.

I arrived at the emergency within minutes after the ambulance carrying Juan arrived at the emergency room entrance.

Gary and the other paramedic had begun unloading Juan to take him inside. I could see a slight grin on Gary's face. As I looked at Juan lying on the stretcher, he was breathing on his own without being bagged or on the ventilator.

"Oh, wow," I said.

"You were right, Jackie, every time I attempted to give him breaths with the ambu bag, he would resist, and his oxygen saturation would drop," Gary said.

"But when I allowed him to breathe on his own, his oxygen level remained one hundred percent. He rode the majority of the trip here breathing on his own."

I praised God for another miracle. It would be the first time that the doctors saw that Juan could breathe some without the ventilator. They rolled Juan into the emergency room where everyone watched in awe as he proved that he was very much alive. He spent the next three hours off his ventilator breathing on his own.

God says that those who believe in Him will never be put to shame. It would be those who did not believe who would be made shame.

I was beginning to wonder about the Juan's Law bill in the House of Representatives. The 2003 legislative session was nearing its end and I had not heard from them. I started sending e-mails to the state representatives to remind them of Senate Bill Twenty-Four, Juan's Law. Representative Billy Mitchell had taken hold of the bill in the House. He assured me that the bill would be voted on during that session.

Representative Mitchell had also introduced a similar bill requiring daycare centers in Georgia to have insurance. Because our bills were similar he chose to go with mine, because we both knew trying to impose insurance was a greater task than disclosure.

Representative Mitchell added an amendment to Senate Bill Twenty-Four that required the Department of Human Resources to recommend insurance when people came in to apply for a child daycare license. This amendment did not go well with Senator Cheeks, who introduced the bill. I prayed constantly that God would stay in the front and in the midst and see it through. He was with me all the way.

I soon had found another nursing company to take over from the company that would not feed Juan. Frances signed on to continue her care for Juan. She truly lived up to her part as a godmother. She was there for me and my family in more ways than one. We were once again on track with our nursing.

Anthony came to visit another time to cut Juan's hair. Anthony seemed a little more positive than before. I often prayed that God would somehow some way soften Anthony's heart. It had been several months since the first time he cut Juan's hair.

"Hey, Daddy's little man," Anthony said as he bent down and kissed Juan.

I stood back not really knowing how to take this but I did it like I did every thing else: I counted it as joy and praised God silently for it.

He did not cut Juan's hair but said he came by to make a promise to come back later and cut it. His visit was very short, but a lot sweeter than the other few he had made.

Juan was soon to celebrate his third birthday. A milestone for him because one doctor said he would be dead by age two. I am so glad that I know that God is the author and finisher of Juan's faith.

As I continued to research daycare centers and liability insurance I found that were a large number of states that were just like Georgia when it came to this issue. I was so sure that many parents were just like me, under assumption that state-licensed child day care facilities. I prayed every day for God to show me a way to make a difference in the lives of someone else who may be faced with what I was going through.

I was sitting at home watching television as my heart throbbed over the fact that it was the last day of the legislative session and Senate Bill Twenty-Four had not come up for a vote. I could only hope that it would as Representative Mitchell had assured me. About an hour, later I received a telephone call.

"May I speak with Jackie Boatwright?" the voice on the other end said.

"This is Jackie," I replied.

"This is Representative Billy Mitchell. The House just passed your bill," he said.

"Oh, my God! You are kidding!" I said. I could hear the sounds of the bells after votes were cast. I remember the sound from my being in the visitor's gallery when the Senate voted on the bill.

"I just thought I would let you know," he said.

"What happens next?" I asked.

"Well you know we added the amendment. The amendment is a requirement by the members of the House for the department who issues child daycare licenses to recommend to people seeking a license to get insurance. We have sent the bill back to the Senate for vote on the amendment, but as of now it is a done deal in the House." He said.

"Thank you so much. This is a very happy day for me and for Juan." I said in joy.

I hung up the phone and gave praise to Our Lord and Savior, because I knew that this had to be His work.

My joy was short lived. I would later find out that because of the amendment Representative Mitchell and the House members added to the bill, it had to be sent back over to the Senate for a re-vote. This did not set well with Senator Cheeks, so he did not bring the bill back up for vote during the last hour of session, which meant that I would have to wait until the next year for the bill to be voted on by the Senate. I still praised God. The old saying "I know He did not bring me this far to leave me now," became my theme.

God will never bring you to the mountain and not take you over. Sometimes you must learn to wait, because when He takes you over, you will never have to worry about crossing over that mountain again.

Juan celebrated his third birthday, and we rejoiced for his being here to see another year. Our celebration was very quiet at home. Many people I thought had forgotten his birthday sent cards wishing him well. I can only tell you in words, because my heart cannot explain what it felt when I stood next to his bed seeing the glory and beauty of God in what we as humans so often think is a man's world.

One night I was lying in bed when my telephone rang. It was a man asking me not to hang up.

"Miss Boatwright, I know that it is late, but I feel that this is some form of divine intervention. I came across your son's Web page while I was viewing another Web page." He said.

"I work for a doctor in Cumming, Georgia. We provide therapy treatments that may benefit your son," he said.

"Sir, I am not interested," I said.

"Please let me explain," he pleaded.

"Okay, I am listening," I responded.

"Have you ever heard of hyperbaric oxygen?" he asked.

"Yes; it has something to do with divers. That is about all that I know."

"Well, it is also used to treat patients who have suffered from near drowning like your son. I do not care, Miss Boatwright, if you choose not to get these treatments with our facility, like I said, I believe my coming across your son's Web page was divine intervention. I saw your address on the Web page and would like to send you some information." he said.

"That will be fine." I hung up the phone wondering where God was getting ready to take us. The next day I spent hours on the Internet researching the procedure and was intrigued with the possibilities. I was more intrigued when I thought about God being in charge of the procedure and what it would do for Juan. One drawback was that it was not covered by Medicaid and it was very expense to have done.

The doctor from Cumming had told me during his conversation the night before that people are placed in the chamber, their bodies are saturated with pure oxygen, and after treatment it had been documented that the body grows new cells; and in near drowning cases, possible new brain cell growth. I found out that divers are sent to the hyperbaric oxygen chamber after they have gone too deep in water causing them to be paralyzed. After several treatments in the oxygen chamber they are able to walk again.

A friend said that they had a hyperbaric facility at Fort Gordon, the military base that was ten minutes away from my house. I had a plan. I

114

wasn't quite sure if it was going to work, but I really wanted Juan to have the treatments after researching and praying about it.

I drove to the base. Getting on the base after September 11 was a task. I could see the soldiers standing like perfect stature as they stopped each car approaching. I drove to the gate and stopped.

"Ma'am, where are you headed today?" the soldier at the gate asked.

"I am going to the hyperbaric chamber."

"Who are you going to see?" he asked.

"I don't know yet. I am hoping to see whoever will see me at that facility."

He looked at me and paused as he pondered what to do. "Ma'am, can you step out of the vehicle and open your trunk and your hood?" he asked.

"Why? Is everything okay?"

"This is just procedure Ma'am."

He was telling the truth, because every car behind me had its trunk and hood open. After he viewed my vehicle, he motioned for me to go through. I had been told that the chamber facility was located near the Eisenhower Hospital. I knew where the hospital was because Juan had been there during his initial accident and after his second code.

I slowly opened the heavy door. My eyes scanned the room, and my mouth hung slightly opened. I had never seen any medical equipment such as that one. There were two very large cylinders that occupied the majority of the space in the room.

"May I help you, Ma'am?" a soldier asked.

"Yes I would like to speak with whom ever is in charge." I said.

"That would be Dr. Boyle. I will see if he is available."

He went to see if the doctor would speak with me. I thought, Lord, please help me say the right thing, because I am sort of lost for words at this point.

A doctor came out. "Hi, I am Dr. Boyle. How can I help you?" He said as he extended his hand.

"Well, I am not sure if you can help me, but I am hoping that you can." I said as I shook his hand.

He led me into his office and asked me to take a seat.

"I came here because I have a child who suffered a near drowning. I have spent the last few days researching hyperbaric oxygen, and I would like my son to receive the treatments. To be honest, sir, I do not have any money, and I know these treatments are expensive, but I was wondering if I allowed you to treat my son and use it as a study for future treatments, if I could get it done at no cost." My heart raced.

"Wow! I don't know. Nobody has ever asked me such a question. Are you military?"

"No, we are not," I said.

"I don't know if the Army would be willing to take on the risk because you are not military."

I reached into my purse and pulled out a picture of Juan.

"Sir, this is my son, and if there is something out there that God has created that can help him, I am pleading with you help us."

"Please don't get me wrong. If it were up to me I would say 'when do we start.' But I need to find out who I need to get approval from. I will call you in a few days after I look into it," he said.

"Sure."

I gave him my telephone number and I left not realizing that this man would become a major part of the plan God had for Juan..

Sure enough he called later that week.

"I spoke with my boss, and we have to get approval from the Secretary of the Army before we can do this." He said. "There is no guarantee he is going to say yes. I am willing to bet that he will say no, but it won't hurt us to ask."

"That is all I can ask for, a yes or no." I responded.

He asked me to write a letter about what happened to my son and to explain our financial situation. He said he was going to take care of putting together the main plan of action to present to the secretary of the Army. We decided to talk again in a few weeks or before if he heard something sooner. I prayed that God would soften the hearts of those who were the decision makers in this situation.

Juan's story was reaching more and more people. I was being asked to share his story at area churches. The good news of God and his love was spreading as people shared in my faith. Some of them could not understand where my faith came from or how I was able to withstand all that we had gone through.

God is truly faithful and able to do anything but fail us. The key to our prayers is our faith. The Bible says in Hebrews that through faith kingdoms were subdued, promises were obtained, and the mouths of lions were stopped. Not only that, women received their dead raised to life, and people escaped the edge of the sword all out of faith.

When I tell you that I believe that Jesus raised Lazarus from the dead, I believe it with all that is in me. That is why I stand so firmly on His raising Juan up to be completely whole.

Many people have asked if I am referring to a spiritual healing. I am shocked that people do not believe that God can in this day and age heal us physically. When God healed in the biblical days, those people were physically healed. If you believe in God like you say you do, why would you allow someone to make you think that expecting a healing from God means only a spiritual healing?

God has not changed. He is the same God today as He was then, and if he did it for them, I can assure you that He can and will do it for you, if your faith is where it should be.

Chapter 7

I know that God is going to raise Juan up for the world to see, and when that day comes, what a glorious day in the name of the Lord that will be!

Christians forget that they are heirs to the promises of God. When God made the covenant with Abraham, Isaac, and Jacob, that inheritance was passed on to us. Many of us think that God thinks as we do. Isaiah 55:8-9 says *"For my thoughts are not your thoughts, neither are your ways my ways, saith the Lord. For as the heavens are higher than the earth, so are my ways higher than your ways, and my thoughts than your thoughts."*

We have put God into a box attempting to limit what he is able to do. Many people thought God would not heal my son. I am thankful that I thought otherwise. Man cannot heal Juan but God was going use Juan to heal man, spiritually.

A few months passed before I received the news from Dr. Boyle that the secretary of the army declined to allow Juan to have hyperbaric treatments done as a study at Fort Gordon. At first I was a little broken, but I knew that if God was for it, then it was only a minor issue, and God would prepare another way.

I started calling the local hospitals to find out if they provided hyperbaric treatments and if so how much would it cost. I was fortunate to get a hospital that was willing to work with me on the cost. I considered it to be a blessing. I was even more blessed when Dr. Boyle, who specialized in hyperbaric medicine, agreed out of the kindness of his heart to attend the initial meeting with the doctor to help me answer any questions I had.

You see God will send an angel as you wait, to assist you with whatever your needs may be. Dr. Boyle was our angel. His knowledge was priceless, and for some reason his mere being there gave me a sense of peace about the procedure.

After leaving the doctor's office I knew that getting the money to get started was something I had to put in the hands of God. I was not working, had not worked in two years, and was standing on my faith for God to provide the money for Juan's treatments. I needed five thousand two hundred dollars.

My girlfriends and I came up with several fund-raising ideas. The only one we actually carried out was a yard sale. That Saturday was one of the most beautiful times my girlfriends and I had together. It was a very brisk morning. Jennifer, Shirley, Dot and Theracia had been supportive of everything I did for Juan and had been supportive of my faith. I truly thanked God for them. They all got up very early to travel a long distance to be there for that day. Although the weather was cold, our time together was very warm and memorable.

They all opened up their closets and homes to donate things for the yard sale. We never laughed so hard as we did at some of the things we had in our closets that were outdated. One item Jennifer had bought was a prom dress from the mid-1980s. We could not believe she still had such a dress. I laughed out loud when Dot opened a box of shoes, and she had the military style boots that were also classic 1980s.

"Oh my God look at these things." I said holding them in the air.

I don't think any of us could hold back our laughter. We raised few hundred dollars from that day. Jennifer's prom dress and Dot's army boots did not sell, but we had a great time sneaking them into the back of Shirley's truck with a note expressing how good we thought she would look in her new outfit. You should have heard her when she realized she had taken those items home with her. Now that was funny!

We were still a long way from the five thousand two hundred we needed to start the treatments. I had posted the fund-raising on Juan's web page. A few dollars came in from that. Our fund-raising was going very slowly and our schedules began to conflict. I wondered if I was ever going to be able to raise the money I needed to start the treatments.

Well God soon answered. It was a few months later that I received a telephone call from a woman stating she had read my book and heard me speak at a function. She told me I strengthened her faith like it had never been strengthened before and she saw on Juan's website I was trying to raise money for the hyperbaric oxygen treatments. Her next statement really touched me. She wanted to know where to mail a check to pay for the treatments in full. God is surely a great God. On our second visit I would find out that God had some other plans for me. The hyperbaric oxygen facility was located next to the ICU burn unit at the hospital. One morning I was unloading Juan from the van to take him into the hospital for his treatments when a woman approached me and asked if I would come and pray for her infant daughter who had developed mysterious burns on various areas of her body.

Totally caught off guard, again I pondered why this woman who I do not know and who doesn't know me, would ask me to pray for her daughter. Needless to say, I agreed. A few days later, we arrived at the hospital for another treatment for Juan and there were at least six other families waiting for me to pray for their loved ones. The little baby, through only the grace of God, made a miraculous recovery. The mother had shared with the others that I'd prayed for her. So for the next eighty days the nurse and I took Juan for treatments, after getting him into the chamber, I went over to the burn unit to pray for those who requested prayer.

Juan's Story, my self-published book, touched the hearts of many people, leading several back to Christ and several to Him for the first time. I was stunned to receive an e-mail from Iraq, considering since we were at war. My book had reached that far. A solider from Augusta who I would later find out, was a minister was sent the book, and he was kind enough to share with me how much it blessed him during his tour of duty.

He told me that his unit even used my book as the subject for one of their Sunday morning church services. This is one of his many e-mails that inspired me to keep on fighting the good fight for the Lord.

"Jackie, hi again. I'm sorry; I began to tell you about the book a while ago, but I never finished the message. I enjoyed it from the minister's prospective of reading about how you continued to lean and depend on God, even in the face of the doctors and everyone else telling you to give up. I also thoroughly enjoyed how you began putting God in remembrance of His word and you didn't let what your eyes saw keep you from speaking what your heart knows. I preached a message recently titled, "Whom Do You Believe: God or Your Lying Eyes?" It was basically dealing with living life from a faith point of view; the faith that tells you to believe and trust God, and not what your eyes are telling you. Since the eyes are the points that the devil likes to use to attack us, sometimes he'll try to let what our eyes are seeing keep us from believing what God has already said. You, on the other hand, chose to believe and quote God at His word, and to not let the things that were (and are) going on around you keep you from speaking His word.

He tells us to put Him in remembrance of His word,

but sometimes we wonder, "Why? Isn't God already omniscient? Doesn't He already know, what's He's said?" Yes, He does, but when we begin to speak the same things that He has already spoken, then those things that are not, shall come to pass! His word has already declared it, and I'm just bold enough to take Him at His word. I marvel at the courage and determination of mothers; you all have a type of love for your children that is unmatched by any father except God.

A mother's love goes beyond the point of pain, and sticks with the child even after the children are back on their feet, going about their lives. The love you show for Juan (and Derek) is awesome in and of itself. It could only have come from God! One other person has already read the book, and another is currently in the midst of it. I'm hoping that it will inspire and encourage others to keep their hands in God's hands, no matter how dire the situation may look.

There's one guy over here that saw the book and said that he's related to you in some manner; I believe his name is Bobby Steele. Small world, isn't it? I'm also glad to hear that you're in no financial strain; God has a way of making sure that His people are taken care of. As David said in Psalm 37, "I have been young, and now am old; yet never have I seen the righteous forsaken, nor his seed begging bread." You continue to be encouraged, and continue to spread the Gospel through your testimonies. Thank you for the prayers that you, Juan, and Derek are sending up for us. You may thank us, but I thank you for thinking of us and keeping us lifted up in prayer. In Christ, Ian

I would later receive an e-mail from South Africa, from a man bearing the same name as the soldier, I just told you about. The man from Africa praised me for my faith and said he and his family also planned to share Juan's story with churches there. You see when God has a purpose and a plan, He works in wondrous and mysterious ways. When God raises Juan up, the world will see that God is God all by himself, and people will know that He has not changed, and that He is truly able to do all things.

God has a way of handling every situation that we encounter and He says that vengeance belongs to Him, so please allow him to do what He does best in. Anthony and Cheryl continued their negative treatment towards Juan. Anthony was doing everything he could to avoid paying child support, and Cheryl continued spreading noxious rumors about my Juan and his condition, even going so far as to say that Juan was dead and that she buried him.

Cheryl did not know that Anthony was calling me seeking direction on so many things. One thing Anthony knew about me was that I was spiritually connected and even after he had gotten married, a part of him for some reason or another relied on me for guidance in that area. When I was calling him about child support, he would find a way to share with me his burdens. During one conversation, he told me that right after he had gotten married he cried uncontrollably for two weeks as Cheryl frantically went out trying to buy him things, to ease his turmoil.

Another conversation evolved into him telling me that he was not happy and his new bride did not turn him on. I guess one of the more shocking things he said was that he truly desired to spend time with his kids, and that he finally told her if he could not be a father to his kids, he could not be a husband to her. I would always tell him that he needed to pray. I needed my child support money. If truth be told, a part of me was feeling and thinking that he was getting what he deserved; however, I knew that was not a God-like thought. So I often prayed with him and for him.

Needless to say, I gave up and turned that situation totally into the hands of God to deal with as He felt necessary. In essence, I stopped all communications with Anthony and vowed that I was not going to waste another day trying to get him to take care of his child who so desperately needed him. Anthony's life would soon start a downward spiral. One morning I had an early morning health department appointment to pick up some vouchers for Juan. I grabbed my morning paper and jumped into my car. I began reading the newspaper as I was waiting for my name to be called. Anthony's name jumped off the paper at me. When I met Anthony, he was a sheriff's deputy in Augusta. I sat with my jaw hanging open as I read, the headline, Man jailed for impersonating a police officer.

The paper said that Anthony was out at a club at around two in the morning. The club had a wet T-shirt contest, and Anthony was accused of touching the women inappropriately and was confronted by the club's security officer and later asked to leave. In all of the commotion, Anthony apparently told the security officer that he could have him arrested because he was a deputy, and he flashed his old ID card to support his claim.

The incident would later cause him to become the butt of many jokes as radio personalities made humorous jokes about the incident daily for the next week. In some twisted way, I felt sorry for him because I knew how highly he thought of himself, and now his face was being flashed on all of the local news channels because impersonating a police officer is illegal in Georgia.

Several months had passed before God would speak to me concerning Anthony after that incident. One morning, in early December, I was going to pick up Juan's medical supplies when I heard the Holy Spirit speak. I was reaching for my keys that were lying on my dresser, I heard God's voice.

"Jackie, you need to call Anthony, you need to give him one more chance." The Lord said.

"My God, I have not talked to Anthony for months now. Give him one more chance at what?" I asked as I stood there listening attentively.

"Call him," the Lord responded.

I really was not sure what was going on, but I knew that obedience had been a major factor in my faith, and I was not about to start disobeying God. I dialed Anthony's work number. He worked as a car salesman for local car dealership. When the operator answered, I asked to be transferred to his desk.

"This is Anthony, how may I help you," he said naturally assuming it was a sales call.

'Hi, Anthony, this is Jackie. How are you?"

"I'm fine." He responded.

"I was calling to see if we could talk." I added

"I don't have any money," he responded.

"Anthony, I did not call you about money, I called you about Juan. We have a child who is sick and needs both of his parents," I said calmly.

"Is he all right," he asked.

"He is fine. Can we meet somewhere for lunch?"

After hesitating, he finally agreed. We were going to meet at a restaurant that was mid point for both of us. While driving there, I was very nervous because, I had no idea what God was going to have me say to him, and even more, how he was going to respond. I pulled into the parking lot. Anthony was not there yet so I sat praying silently to God. A

126

few moments later, I saw his Lincoln Navigator drive into the parking lot. I got out of my car and headed for the restaurant. Anthony caught up to me before I made it to the door. We greeted each other with a casual hello and he reached and opened the door for me.

After we were seated and had ordered our meals, our conversation with each other began.

"Anthony, I came here to give you one last chance to be a father to your son." I said, and I knew those were not my words; they were God's words.

"I don't have time."

I looked in shock at his response, and my thoughts were interrupted, as clear liquid trickled from his nose.

"Are you sick? You know my stomach is weak; and you need to go to the restroom and clean your nose." I said with a harsh tone and a negative attitude.

"I am sorry. I have been dealing with this cold thing." He grabbed a napkin and headed for the men's room. He returned shortly.

"Where were we?" he asked.

Before I could answer his question, the waitress came over and took our food and drink orders.

"I told you I came here to give you a final chance to be a father to your son, and you told me you did not have time," I said.

"Jackie, my life is full. I am working all the time, and when I get home, Cheryl has a long list of things she wants me to do. I would love to spend time with my son, but I just don't have the time." He twisted his finger into his temple.

"That is all well and good, but you need to find time for your son. I have a lot to do as well, but I know that if Juan ever needed me, he needs me now, and he needs you too. As long as he knows we are there for him,

127

he will keep fighting to live."

"If you had never-" He started to say.

"Anthony, I did not come here to go back over the past." I said, interrupting him.

I thought the conversation would change when the waitress brought our food to the table.

"Well, we could have been together, and I -." He began again.

"Anthony, stop. I have moved on, and it is obvious you have. You are married now. All I want is what is best for Juan. And for whatever it is worth, if I did anything hurtful to you, I apologize, and ask that you forgive me." I said.

He sat quietly looking at me. "I forgive you. And if I did anything to hurt you, please forgive me." I he said

"You are forgiven." I said. "Now again, I came here to give you a final chance to be a father to Juan."

"Jackie, I told you I don't have a lot of time but I will see what I can do."

"One day you won't have anything but time, and remember, when I leave here today, you won't have another chance."

Neither of us ate much of the food on our plates. Anthony sat there quiet, as though meditating on what I said. As always he would say something to try to make me laugh.

"Are you paying for this?"

"Are you insane?" I responded.

Signally the waitress, I asked for the check.

"Together or separate?" she asked.

"Definitely separate," I said.

We left the restaurant on a peaceful note. I did not know that would be the last time I would see him alive. The next week he was shot seven times and killed.

It was the early morning of December 11, when my door bell rang around 4:00. I stumbled sleepily to the door. "Who is it?" I asked

"Jackie, it's Frances. Open the door."

I opened the door and tiredly fell back on the couch. She came into my living room wearing her paramedic uniform.

"What are you doing here this time of morning?" I asked.

"I came to tell you that Anthony is dead."

"Anthony who?"

"Anthony Boatwright," She said mistakenly.

I quickly awoke and jumped up to run toward Juan's room, when she grabbed me by the arm stopping me.

"I am sorry, I mean Anthony Cobb," she said softly.

Frances, a paramedic supervisor, was at the scene of Anthony's death.

Obviously stunned, I stood motionless and silent. I sat down on the couch, for I was finding it difficult to believe what she was telling me.

I would later find out what happened. It appears he was a victim of a double homicide. Not only was he killed but the woman he was with was shot too. Although Anthony was married, he was having an affair with another woman, and the woman's ex-boyfriend broke into the house, from what it looks like, and shot and killed him and her. Anthony's body was found in the yard of a neighboring house a couple of doors down.

Oh, my God, it was very surreal to me, hearing all of this knowing that I had just met with him a few days before. At the moment I was thinking of asking God why, He reminded me that He had offered Anthony another chance at life through me but he refused.

The morning news brought more irony. On the top half of the front page was the news of Anthony's death; on the bottom half of the same page was the story about the judgment awarded in Juan's case against

Maria. The astounding part to this was Anthony was thirty-three years old at the time of his death, and Juan was awarded thirty-three million dollars.

The local television stations were buzzing after learning that the male victim was Juan's father. One station sent a reporter to my house to seek an interview. I shared with him that Anthony had a wife, and maybe he should speak with her, he told me that they were more concerned with my thoughts, especially with my faith, and now that this had happened in addition to Juan's accident.

The story aired along with old photos of Anthony and me, which upset Cheryl. I am sure she was embarrassed that the entire city knew Anthony was not faithful to her, and now the television stations were more concerned about my thoughts and feelings than they were hers. The reporter called me and told me that she telephoned the station and accused me of trying to make the public think I was Anthony's wife. I never quite understood why she would think that I would want to give that impression, especially the circumstances under which he died.

The reporter told me he informed her that what she was alleging was not true because it was me who told them that he was married, and I even sent my condolences out to her during the interview. He added he allowed her to listen to the audio of the interview again. She tried to say negative things about me, but he told her he was not interested.

I guess because she could not lash out and get results with the television station, she took it a step further. Cheryl sent word to me that she did not want me to bring Juan to Anthony's funeral, and if I did, she said what she was going to do to me. At first I was sincerely bothered, but being a woman of God, I knew that to disrespect His house would not be pleasing to Him, and at this time, I surely did not want to disrespect Anthony's parents and siblings, who were already emotionally broken, with Anthony's untimely death. So I opted to take Juan to the funeral home to say his good-byes to his father.

Many people felt that I should have been happy about what had happened to Anthony. One woman got angry at me because I told her I received no joy in the death of my son's father regardless of his and my differences. She accused me of still being in love with him as the reason why I did not gloat his demise.

No matter what Anthony may have or have not done, I did not believe anyone should be brutally murdered in the manner in which he had been killed. God loves the unjust just as much as he does the just. As a matter of fact, God would later reveal to me in a dream that Anthony made it to heaven.

Juan had been unable to have a bowel movement for about a week. I had been giving him laxatives and enemas, but none of them were working. The night before I decided to take Juan to the hospital, his heart rate had reached close to one hundred and ninety. I prayed to God for help. I spent hours rubbing Juan's stomach to ease his discomfort. From the corner's of my eye I could see glimpses of black shadows passing Juan's doorway. I continued praying to God as I rubbed his stomach.

I could not understand why my prayers were not getting through.

"Juan something is wrong because when Mommy prays God hears and answers," I said rubbing his stomach.

I was so tired. I had been up with him most of the night. I looked at the clock. It was three o'clock in the morning. The more I rubbed Juan's stomach, his heart rate lowered. Seeing that he was settling down, I went into my bedroom to catch a quick nap, before the alarms on his machines went off again. As soon as my head fell back on my pillow, I began to dream.

In my dream, a demon kicks open my door and he is looking for Anthony. The demon asks me to tell him where Anthony is. I kept telling him I did not know. He began to kick me and punch me. Suddenly, the demon disappears. I hear a knock on the door and it is Anthony. As I started to tell him what had just happened, I was attempting to close the door when another demon forcefully pushed the door open. The demon and Anthony began to fight. In my dream I could hear them knocking over furniture and hitting the walls.

I heard Anthony tell the demon if he did not let go of him, he was going to kill him. I screamed to Anthony to kill him. He did. In this dream, I ran and got underneath my bed. As I lay there on my stomach, I could see a woman's legs. She was wearing red high heels. I watched as she paced back and forth in front of my bed. Anthony entered the bedroom, she and he began to fight. After a long battle Anthony destroyed her too. It was only a few seconds later that the first demon came back. He and Anthony began to fight. Their fight was harder and longer than the other two.

They fought until Anthony was down on his knees, sitting back on his heels, and the demon was laying on his stomach. I watched from underneath the bed, as the demon removed a long sword and began to stab Anthony in his stomach. Anthony did not flinch. The demon looked in my direction and removed his sword and began to stab at me under the bed. I slid backward to get out of the way of the blade. Anthony took out a long drill and killed the demon by drilling it into his head. In my dream I heard Anthony ask me if I were okay.

I woke wide awake. I ran into Juan's room to find that he had passed a very large stool. I realized that the black shadows I had been seeing were the demons. The Lord revealed that they could not get to Juan because they were in battle with Anthony. In the bible, the Pharisees accused Jesus of casting out demons in the name of the devil. Jesus told them a house divided cannot stand. If he had cast out devils in the name of the devil, that would be a house divided. Based on this scripture, if Anthony was among the demons, he would not have killed them.

Daniel had been praying constantly to God and he didn't his prayer was going to be answered. When the angel arrived, he told Daniel that his prayer was answered the moment he prayed, but he had to fight with the devil for twenty-one days before he could arrive with the answer to Daniel's prayer.

Jesus also reminded me of when He was dying on the cross. He was between two of the worst criminals of that time period. One of them asked that he be remembered by Jesus when he got to heaven. Jesus stopped dying and said surely on this day, you will be with me in paradise.

The Lord revealed to me that even up to the last minute, everyone has a chance to make Christ their personal savior and enter into the kingdom of heaven. This is why I believe Anthony made it to heaven.

The new year again placed me at the steps of the Capitol in Atlanta. I was elated to learn that the bill had been brought back up for vote in the Senate, and it passed. I could not believe I was on my way into the governor's office to watch him sign the bill into law. I had asked Richard to be there with me.

On my way down the long corridor, I silently praised God for what only he had done. I arrived to find State Representatives Henry Howard and Billy Mitchell waiting to take me into the governor's office. As we were entering the office I was stopped by a reporter.

"How is Juan, Ms. Boatwright?" The reported asked.

"He is fine. I kissed him all over his face and told him that today was not going to be a typical day." I responded.

"How do you feel about all that you have done?" He asked.

"It is not about me, it is about Juan. It is more of his celebration than it is mine. He paid the ultimate price." I said.

I was moved forward and I was greeted by the governor.

"I know this certainly brings back some memories, but it will bring some help for other children." he told me and held my hand.

The governor asked Representative Mitchell to give him the history of the bill and afterwards, he took his monogrammed pen and signed the bill into law. My eyes filled with tears because the new law truly brought validation to Juan's tragedy. The governor handed me the pen he signed the bill with.

My fight did not end with Georgia. I was determined that the other 42 states that did not require child daycare centers to carry liability insurance would also pass Juan's Law. I traveled to the Capitol in Richmond, Virginia, after I persuaded Senator John Edwards to introduce Juan's Law.

I walked into the room full of Senators to convince them to vote yes for Juan's Law. So impressed with my efforts and my story, Senator Edwards passed out copies of a recent article that was written about me by Money Magazine. This obviously impressed the Senators because one asked what my connection was to the state of Virginia. I shared with them that I had an MBA from a university in Virginia. After a few more personal questions, I was allowed to share my viewpoint on the importance of Juan's Law for the children in Virginia. They all voted yes to Juan's Law.

As I was leaving the meeting a woman from the crowd stopped me. "Ms. Boatwright, have you ever considered a career in politics? You were great up there," she said.

"No, I am content with being a mother to Juan, but thank you so much for the compliment." I smiled.

"Think about it; we need more people like you," she added as I was walking away.

Coming down the Capitol steps I heard another female voice calling my name. I stopped and turned in the direction of the voice.

"Ms. Boatwright, wait," she said.

"Yes?." I responded.

"I just wanted you to know that what you are doing for the children of our country is great. I have my own daycare horror. My brother was buried alive at his daycare center," she said tearfully.

Reaching to embrace her, I thanked her. I would return to Virginia a few months later and watch as the state's Governor signed Juan's Law.

My fight would finally end up on the steps of the United States Capitol. I persuaded Congressman John Barrow to introduce The Anthony DeJuan Boatwright Act. The law was introduced on March 12, 2007, if passed, this law will require the remaining forty states to implement Juan's Law. The states that do not implement Juan's Law will not receive federal funding for daycare centers in their state under the Childcare Block Grant.

I knew going in, that Maria would never be able to pay the thirty-three million dollar judgment that was award to Juan by the court. I filed to show lawmakers the financial impact tragedies such as the one Juan suffered, could have on our economy. As of my writing this book, Juan is seven years old and continuing to improve. Dereck has since graduated high school and looking forward to college and I am still trusting God in every thing that I do. The man who murdered Anthony was sentenced to life in prison without the chance of parole.

Before I end, please allow me to clarify some things. I do not think I have any special powers. I do believe that God has found favor in me and has chosen me as a vessel to show His Self.

The book of Mark Chapter Sixteen verses fifteen through eighteen says, *"And He said unto them, Go ye into all the world, and preach the gospel to every creature. He that believeth and is baptized shall be saved; but he that believeth not shall be damned. And these things shall follow them that believe; In My name shall they cast out devils; they shall speak with new tongues; they shall take up*

135

serpents and if they drink any deadly thing, it shall not hurt them; they shall lay hands on the sick, and they shall recover."

It has been through my faith in God that Juan is still alive and that the people I prayed for have been healed, it is not through anything I have done, can do, or ever will be able to do.

I believe in the Word of God with my whole heart. There are times when I get afraid. In those times, I look upon my faith to get me through.

Many people have asked me where my strength comes from. My answer will always be the same: God. He will never put more on you than you can bear, if you trust him.

I trust God and I constantly remind him of his promises. I could have never imagined God using me, and to this day I am still puzzled, but I am also grateful that God sees my heart.

Many people I have met have a tremendous amount of faith but they lack the ability to stand on that faith in their darkest hours. It is when you can stand the test, when it seems there is no hope or no way out of a situation, when God will open the windows of heaven and your miracles will manifest.

Juan's life continued because of my faith in God's promises. Everybody that Jesus healed received the healing because of their faith in what they were asking God to do. Lazarus was raised from the dead because his family *believed* that if Jesus would have been there, he would not have died. The woman with the issue of blood was healed because she *believed* if she could just touch the hem of Jesus' garment, she would be made whole. It was faith that brought Abraham, Moses, Daniel, and the Hebrew Boys through their situations.

I had to learn that God works in his own timing. I am forever reminded of the old adage; whatever is worth having is worth waiting for. Use that when you ask God for whatever you may need and wait for Him to give it to you.

My Darling Son, I know now who you are.

Just the other night, when I was braiding your hair, The Lord spoke to me and said "never cut it, *Like Samson,* his strength lies there.

As you lay across my lap and I gazed at the changes your body had made, my heart hurt with every unnatural twist of your limbs, but the Lord spoke again and said, *Like Job,* I will make them like new; the limbs you see now will not stay with him.

Then I said to myself, you must be the bravest little boy in the whole wide world to take on such a task and stand. The Lord said, *Like David,* with a sling shot and some rocks, he slayed Goliath with his bare hands.

My heart felt overjoyed knowing the many lives you have touched around the world, from the US to Iraq to Africa you are now known. The Lord said, *Like Paul,* he had to travel to spread the Good news that Jesus Christ is Lord alone.

My Darling Son I now, know who you are. And your mission is almost complete, for the Lord spoke to me and promised that soon you will be on your feet. He told me that soon, you would tell the world that Christ is alive and well, and those who don't find Him will surely find the gates of hell. He said that we would have our lives as it was before, but only with an abundance of blessings, for the faith we kept during our troubles in Christ Jesus, whom we adore.

To Juan
From Mommy,

Mastering Faith

Standing on faith is a task that even the most saved Christians often fail to master. The Bible defines faith as "the substance of things hoped for, and the evidence of things not seen," still most who claim to have it often tend to be looking for it. As a woman who has lived this scripture, I can tell you the situation with Juan has taught me how to master faith. I read that scripture over and over again, praying for an understanding that would allow me to exercise this thing called *faith,* the only thing that truly pleases God. The Bible says. "It was by faith that Abraham was counted as righteous and through this same thing called faith, the worlds were framed."

Each day I stood watching Juan, lying there connected to tubes, unable to speak or move much. In my heart it had to be this thing called faith that would sustain me, because my eyes were showing me otherwise, not withstanding what the doctors were telling me.

Trusting totally in the word of God, I convinced myself that I would not allow my eyes to dictate the outcome I desired for my son. If I had even an inkling of mastering this thing called faith, there had to be some serious changes to various aspects of my life. That included the way I spoke about my son, the way I responded to questions and remarks others had concerning my son, even down to the way I lived my life from one day to the next.

After assessing myself, I found that it was not only my eyes that were giving me the problem of standing on faith; but my ears had a role too.

You see, the Bible says in the book of Romans that faith comes by hearing, meaning that the more we hear something, the more we tend to believe it. It was this revelation that led me to stop listening to what the doctors were telling me in regard to my son. Instead each day I told myself what Juan's life would be like. I spoke life into his situation each and every day, holding on to the fact that the Bible says, faith comes by hearing.

In the initial stages of the accident, when the doctors came around to Juan's room to do their rounds, I either left the room or closed the doors if they were out in the hallway, my way of not having to *hear* anything that went against what I was praying for. The doctors had given me their opinion that Juan would be brain-dead and in a vegetative state for the rest of his life, but the word of God was telling me that there was nothing impossible with faith and that by the stripes of Jesus Christ he was healed. For me to exercise faith, I had to decide who I was going to listen too.

Whose report was I going to believe, man's or God's? The doctor said he would not be able to do anything for the rest of Juan's life, yet the Bible was telling me that no matter how bad Juan's situation appeared, there was absolutely nothing impossible for him. God's report was more in line with what I hoped and desired for my son.

Adam and Eve set a very clear example on how what we hear often dictates our faith or trust in God. When Adam and Eve had sinned by eating the forbidden fruit and were hiding, God asked Adam and Eve why they were hiding.

Adam responded that he was afraid because he was naked. God asked him, "Who *told* you that you were naked?"

They did not know that they were naked until Satan told them, and therefore their nakedness became their focus. As long as they were living in faith and on the Word, they did not realize they were naked.

I applied that same method to my own situation by standing on the scriptures and not on what the doctor's told me. If we as Christians can keep in mind what God says, and not what man says we can have all that God has promised us, and that includes complete healing of the physical body.

God created everything for the good of those who love him; that is scripture. We place so much emphasis on finding a specialist that we forget that doctors are just as human as we are. Many of them are faced with some of the same issues that we are facing, yet we put so much hope in their abilities that we often forget that it is God's hand that is working through them. In mastering faith, your trust must be in God and him alone. We must learn to pray for the people who God has placed in our lives to give us earthly care. So many go under anesthesia with their trust in the degree and the medical facility where we are being treated as opposed to trusting true holder of our fate.

God created the doctors and gave them knowledge; as Christians, mastering faith, please keep this in mind. Ask the doctor's diagnosis and stop asking for his prognosis. The diagnosis will give you direct insight on what you should seek God's help for; however, if you are not strong in your faith, a prognosis will have you planning a funeral.

I know that Juan will live to tell of the good works of the Lord. God has not changed. I am living proof of so many scriptures. I can attest to the fact that God will give you strength in times of weaknesses and he will not place any more on you than you can bear. We must learn how to cast our cares and concerns on him. I pray that after reading Juan's Story you will walk away with a better understanding of faith and how to master it. I pray that you will not give up, even in the worst of times, and that your faith will cause the windows of Heaven to open wide and you will see the beauty and the glory of what true faith can do when exercised.

Police Report provided to me by Investigator Sgt. Richard Roundtree

Case#:	01-181756
Suspect:	N/A
Complainant:	Officer's Report

Victim:	Boatwright, Anthony Dejuan B/M (14months)
	070700 / unknown
	2572 Lincolnton Pkwy
	Hephzibah, Ga. 30815
Incident Type:	Injured Child
Incident Location:	2608 Lincolnton Pkwy
	Hephzibah, Ga. 30815
Incident Date:	090901, Sunday
Investigator:	Richard Roundtree 719

090901 (Sunday)
1345 hours
Investigator Roundtree received a page from Sgt. Bunton. Upon returning said page, Sgt. Bunton advised Investigator Roundtree to respond to 2608 Lincolnton Pkwy. in reference to a 14-month-old infant, later identified as Anthony Boatwright, that was found unconscious in a bucket of bleach saturated mob water. Sgt. Bunton advised that Investigator Tanksley was on the scene and Investigator Nutter was at Eisenhower Medical Center with the child. Investigator Roundtree advised that he would be en route to the scene. Sgt. Bunton also advised that Investigator Piper (CST) was en route to the scene. moved to a neighbor's house.

142

Prior to Investigator Roundtree's arrival on the scene, Investigator Nutter arrived at Eisenhower Medical Center and advised Investigator Roundtree of the following: Inv. Nutter spoke with EMT'S, Leslie Bruce and Rhonda Lanier. Bruce and Lanier advised Inv. Nutter that the child is a B/M, Anthony Dejuan Boatwright (1yoa). Lanier related that Anthony Boatwright was at the residence of Maria Jones and had been found in a bucket of water, mixed with bleach. Lanier related that Anthony Boatwright was non responsive when they arrived and the Engine Company # 18 of the Richmond County Fire Dept. arrived at the same time.

Lanier advised Inv. Nutter that they had received that call at 1233 hrs, arrived at 1239hrs, immediately loaded Anthony Boatwright and arrived at DDEMC at 1255 hours Inv. Nutter walked to the Trauma room and observed that a team of doctors and nurses were performing CPR on Anthony Boatwright. Inv. Nutter was unable to speak with any of the medical staff but was advised that Dr. Bryan Sleigh was the attending physician.

Inv. Nutter went to the Quiet Room where Jones had been placed. Inv. Nutter completed an interview worksheet on Jones and conducted an oral interview. Inv. Nutter notes that Jones is visibly shaken and stated that she was having chest pains. Inv. Nutter advised a clerk that Jones was complaining of chest pains. Inv. Nutter asked Jones if she felt like talking and she agreed to give Inv. Nutter a verbal statement, which consisted of the following:

Jones stated that she runs a daycare and has been keeping Anthony Boatwright since he was two (2) weeks old and keeps four (4) other children. Jones stated that she was keeping Anthony Boatwright for his mother, Jacqueline Boatwright to attend church and Jones does not know what church Jacqueline Boatwright attends.

Jones stated that Jacqueline Boatwright arrived with Anthony Boatwright at 1000 hours Jones stated that she had been cleaning house and had placed the mop bucket in the kitchen. Jones stated that Anthony Boatwright had been following her all around the house and she turned to go to the laundry room and within a few minutes Jones' son screamed at her that he thought Anthony Boatwright had drowned. At this time Jones stated that she could not breathe and Inv. Nutter left the Quiet Room and requested that Jones receive medical attention.

1424 hours

Investigator Roundtree arrived on the scene and met with Investigator Tanksley, Investigator Piper and Sgt. Smith. Investigator Tanksley stated that Montaque Jones advised that he was inside his bedroom when one of the children alerted him that Anthony Boatwright had drowned. Montaque Jones stated that he and his wife rushed to the livingroom and rendered aid to the child. Investigator Tanksley advised that the other children inside the home at the time of the incident were Maria Jones' three children, Demarcos Anderson, Delson Anderson and Dracy Anderson and Maria Jones' two(2) nephews Dwayne Clark and Devonte Smikle. Investigator Tanksley advised that he would conduct a formal interview of Montaque Jones and Sgt. Smith advised that he would start conducting interviews of the children.

Investigator Roundtree also met with Patrol Unit #130 Deputy Herring who advised that he was the first Patrol Unit on the scene. Deputy Herring stated that when he arrived on the scene the Fire Department was standing by and the Ambulance Service had already transported Anthony Boatwright to Eisenhower Medical Center. Deputy Herring stated that he was dispatched at 1251 hours and arrived on the scene 1255 hours

Investigator Roundtree and Investigator Piper entered the residence and began processing the scene. Upon entering the residence Investigator Roundtree noted the livingroom was filled with children's toys to include two(2) cribs, two(2) baby carriers, several play mats and a baby changing station. To the left of the livingroom was a hallway with two(2) bedrooms on the right side of the hallway and one(1) bedroom on the left. The first bedroom on the right side of the hallway had been converted to a den. Walking through the livingroom and entering the kitchen Investigator Roundtree detected a slight odor of bleach consistent with freshly moped floors. The kitchen was well organized with no dishes in the sink and no items appeared to be out of place. To right of the kitchen just prior to entering the hallway, Investigator Roundtree noted a five (5) gallon bucket, which contained approximately two(2) gallons of soiled water, which had a distinct odor of

144

bleach. Investigator Roundtree observed a black child's T-shirt in the sink that had a discoloration from the waist to the neck consistent with being submerged in bleach. The bedroom at the right end of the hallway appeared to be that of a child's, due to the fact that it contained a bunk bed, video game and several toys. The bedroom on the left side of the hall appeared to be the master bedroom, which contained a separate bath. After conducting initial observations, Investigator Piper advised that he would process the scene, to include video and photographs and forward the results to Investigator Roundtree. Investigator Piper advised that he would also collect a sample of the mop water as well as collect the T-shirt that was found in the sink.

1411 hours

Investigator Tanksley conducted an interview with Montaque Jones where he gave a written statement that reflected the following. Jones stated that on 090901 at approximately 1230 hours he was in his bedroom watching the NFL pre game show. Jones stated that his stepson (Delson Anderson) ran into his bedroom and stated "daddy I think Dejuan (Anthony Boatwright) has drowned". Jones stated that he jumped out of the bed and ran through the hallway towards the kitchen.

Jones stated that he heard Maria Anderson scream "Monty". Jones stated that he arrived at the kitchen and pulled Anthony Boatwright out of the bucket. Jones stated that Anthony Boatwright was headfirst in the bucket with his waistline on the edge of the bucket. Jones stated that Anthony Boatwright's head was not touching the water inside the bucket but one of his hands was.

Investigator Tanksley asked Jones why was the bucket in the kitchen and Jones responded that Maria Anderson had just finished mopping the floor. Investigator Tanksley asked Jones what types of chemicals were in the mop water and he answered Clorox bleach and Gain washing powder. Jones stated that he laid Anthony Boatwright on the floor on his back and checked to see if he had a pulse. Investigator Tanksley asked Jones if Anthony Boatwright had a pulse at this time. Jones stated that he did not.

Jones stated that Maria Anderson then asked him to perform CPR on Anthony Boatwright. Jones stated that he squeezed the abdomen of Anthony Boatwright and fluid came out of his mouth and nose.

Jones stated that Maria Anderson then began to administer CPR to the child. Jones stated that one of his children had already dialed 911 and he then talked with the dispatcher and advised them of what had taken place while Maria Anderson was performing CPR. Jones stated that he took over performing CPR on Anthony Boatwright until help arrived. Jones stated that R.C.F.D. arrived shortly after and took over the care of Anthony Boatwright. Investigator Tanksley asked Jones how many people were inside the residence when the incident occurred. Jones answered 8 people total including Anthony Boatwright. Investigator Tanksley asked Jones which of the five children at the residence were his children living at the residence.

Jones answered three and gave there names as follows: Delson Anderson 12yoa 061189, Dracy Anderson 13yoa 062788, and Demarcos Anderson 9yoa 031192 nod. Jones then stated that the other two children were Dwayne Clark and Devonte Smikle. Jones stated that Clark and Smikle were his nephews and they were visiting. Investigator Tanksley asked Jones where was Maria Anderson when Delson Anderson entered the room.

Jones responded that he thought she was in the room with him. Investigator Tanksley asked Jones where were the other children when Delson Anderson entered their room. Jones stated that they all were in the doorway. Investigator Tanksley asked Jones which child actually found Anthony Boatwright. Jones stated Delson Anderson. This concludes the interview with Jones.

1440 hours

Sgt. Smith conducted an audio taped interview with Delson Anderson. Anderson who is 12 yoa stated that he walked into the hallway and saw the victim's Anthony Dejuan Boatwright, waist and legs on the outside of a bucket and Boatwright's upper torso and head inside a mop bucket. Anderson then went and got his 13-year-old brother Dracy Anderson.

Dracy Anderson pulled Boatwright out of the bucket, which contained a combination of water and bleach. Delson Anderson stated that he got his father, Montigue Jones and Jones started CPR. Delson Anderson also stated that everything had been fine in the house and that there had been no problems during the day. Delson Anderson stated that Boatwright had been at the house since 7 or 8 AM. Delson Anderson could not tell if Boatwright was breathing or not when Boatwright was pulled from the bucket.

1455 hours

Sgt. Smith interviewed Dracy Anderson who stated that his brother Delson Anderson came and got him and stated that Boatwright was drowning. Dracy Anderson stated that he then pulled Boatwright out of the bucket and got Jones who then started CPR. Dracy Anderson stated that Delson Anderson called 911 while Jones was performing CPR.

Dracy Anderson was unable to tell if Boatwright was breathing when he was pulled from the bucket but that Boatwright's eyes were closed. Dracy Anderson stated that the bucket was in the hallway next to the kitchen. Dracy Anderson stated that his mother had been mopping floors earlier in the day. Dracy Anderson stated that there had been no problems earlier and that Boatwright was no more mischievous that any one-year-old.

1500 hours

Jacqueline Boatwright arrived at DDEMC and was placed in a waiting area and was advised of the incident by Dr. Sleigh. Jacqueline Boatwright was allowed in the room with Anthony Boatwright. Dr. Sleigh advised Inv. Nutter that Anthony Boatwright was being transported to MCG Children's Medical Center.

1515 hours

Inv. Nutter learned that Jones had been placed in a treatment room to receive treatment for chest pains. Inv. Nutter entered the room and advised Jones to come to CID so a formal interview could be conducted.

1515 hours

Investigator Roundtree met with Dwayne Clark (13yoa) and conducted a taped interview. Clark stated that he and his brother Devonte Smikle (8yoa) arrived at the residence on yesterday. Clark stated that he and

147

his brother spent the night at the residence and when he woke up this morning Anthony Boatwright had arrived at the residence. Clark stated that he did not what time Anthony Boatwright arrived but only that he was not there when he went to sleep last night around 1230 hours

Clark stated that he along with the other children to include Anthony Boatwright were all in the last bedroom on the right side of the hall playing video games. Clark stated that Demarcos Anderson, Delson Anderson and Devonte Smikle left the bedroom and went to the livingrom to play and Anthony Boatwright followed them.

Clark stated that a short time later they all returned to the bedroom and continued to play the video game. Clark stated that at some point Anthony Boatwright must have walked out of the room because one of the other children stated that it was to quiet. Clark stated that Delson Anderson left the room to go and check on Anthony Boatwright. Clark stated that Delson Anderson ran back into the room and yelled that Anthony Boatwright had drowned.

Clark stated that they beat on Maria Jones' door, informed her what had happened and ran into the kitchen. Clark stated that Montaque Jones grabbed Anthony Boatwright and Maria Jones started CPR on Anthony Boatwright. Clark stated that a short time later, EMS arrived at the residence. Clark stated that Maria Jones' and her husband had been inside their room with the door closed for approximately 10 - 15 minutes prior to Delson discovering Anthony Boatwright in the water. See Clark's taped statement for further details.

1521 hours

Investigator Tanksley conducted a taped statement of Demarcos Anderson, which reflected the following. Demarcos Anderson stated that he and the other five children, including Anthony Boatwright, were in the living room playing. Demarcos Anderson stated that all of the older children went to the rear of the residence to play games and forgot that Anthony Boatwright was in the living room alone.

Demarcos Anderson made the statement that he was also supposed to be putting up some clothes. Investigator Tanksley asked Demarcos Anderson where were his parents when they went to the room. Demarcos Anderson stated that they were in their bedroom.

Investigator Tanksley asked Demarcos Anderson to continue

and he stated that Anthony Boatwright was playing in the water and drowned. Investigator Tanksley asked Demarcos Anderson if he saw Anthony Boatwright playing in the bucket of water and he stated no. Investigator Tanksley asked Demarcos Anderson if he has seen Anthony Boatwright if he has seen Anthony Boatwright playing in a bucket of water before and he stated yes. Investigator Tanksley advised Demarcos Anderson that he needed to tell only what he saw today.

Demarcos Anderson then stated that his brother (Delson Anderson) went to the kitchen to get a hammer and found Anthony Boatwright in the bucket. Demarcos Anderson then stated that Delson Anderson ran into the bedroom where they were located and stated that Anthony Boatwright had drowned. Demarcos Anderson further stated that all of the children went to the kitchen and his older brother (Dracy Anderson) pulled Anthony Boatwright from the bucket and held him upside down by his waist attempting to get the water out of his body.

Demarcos Anderson then stated that Dracy Anderson placed Anthony Boatwright on the floor on his back. Demarcos Anderson stated that everyone but Dracy Anderson went to Maria Anderson and Jones' bedroom door. Demarcos Anderson stated that they knocked on the door and his parents asked what they wanted and they stated through the locked door "Anthony Boatwright had drowned. Investigator Tanksley asked Demarcos Anderson if the door to his parent's room was closed and he stated yes. Investigator Tanksley asked Demarcos Anderson if the door was locked and he stated yes. This concludes the interview with Demarcos Anderson.

1530 hours
Investigator Roundtree met with Devonte Smikle (8yoa) and conducted a taped interview. Smikle's statement was consistent with the account given by Clark. Smikle stated that he was inside the bedroom along with the other children playing and before he knew it everyone started running around and yelling. See Smikle's taped statement for further details.

1532 hours

149

Anthony Boatwright was placed in an ambulance and was transported to MCGCMC. Inv. Nutter left DDEMC, en-route to MCGCMC.

1550 hours

Inv. Nutter arrived at MCG Children's Medical Center and was advised that Anthony Boatwright had been placed in Pediatric Intensive Care Unit. Inv. Nutter went to PICU and observed a team of doctors working on Anthony Boatwright. Inv. Nutter learned that the primary physician was Dr. Stephen Papizan.

1600 hours

Investigator Roundtree left the scene and arrived at Engine Company #18 and met with Sgt. Melno. Sgt. Melno stated that his company was dispatched to the scene at 1237 hours and when they arrived on the scene at 1239 hours they found Anthony Boatwright unresponsive with no pulse and not breathing. Sgt. Melno stated that he took over CPR from Maria Jones and the ambulance service arrived and took over care of the child. Sgt. Melno stated that Lt. Milton and Officer Capell also responded to the scene.

1628 hours

Investigator Roundtree arrived at MCG PICU and met with Investigator Nutter. Investigator Nutter advised that Anthony Boatwright was currently being treated by Dr. Stephen Papizan and Anthony Boatwright's mother, Jacqueline Boatwright was inside the treatment room.

Investigator Roundtree briefly met with Jacqueline Boatwright. Jacqueline Boatwright stated that Maria Jones had been recommended to her by a friend as a good child care provider and since the residence was very close to hers, Jacqueline Boatwright stated that Maria Jones started taking care of Anthony Boatwright since he was two(2) weeks old. Jacqueline Boatwright stated that on average, Maria Jones cares for Anthony Boatwright Monday through Friday from approximately 0830 hours to 2030 hours Jacqueline Boatwright stated that on occasion she drops Anthony Boatwright off on Sundays to

150

attend church and that Anthony Boatwright has also spent the night at the residence. Jacqueline Boatwright stated that she called Maria Jones this morning at approximately 0800 hours and asked Maria Jones to keep Anthony Boatwright while she attended church. Jacqueline Boatwright stated that she dropped Anthony Boatwright off at approximately 1000 hours and left for church.

Jacqueline Boatwright stated that Anthony Boatwright was progressing normally for a child his age and suffered from no illnesses or disabilities. Jacqueline Boatwright stated that prior to toady there have been no incidents involving her child's health. Jacqueline Boatwright stated that she has one(1) other child, Derrick Boartwright, 12. Jacqueline Boatwright stated that Anthony Boatwright's father, Ray Cobb lived in Augusta but that they were not together and that she has sole custody of Anthony Boatwright. Jacqueline Boatwright became very emotional and the interview was stopped at that point.

Prior to leaving the PICU, Investigator Roundtree met with Dr. Papizan. Dr. Papizan stated that Anthony Boatwright was in critical condition and was not expected to survive through the night. Dr. Papizan stated that Anthony Boatwright had blood in his lungs and X-rays showed hazing in the chest. Dr. Papizan stated that the hazing in the chest was consistent with drowning but did not normally occur until several days afterwards which would indicate that some form of chemical was inhaled or swallowed. Dr. Papizan stated that is if there was any change in Anthony Boatwright condition he would have someone contact CID.

1720 hours

Jones arrived in CID and Inv. Nutter and conducted an oral interview than was then transposed into a typed statement that reads as follows:
I, Maria Jones operate a daycare center and keep children in my home. I usually keep five (5) children in my home. I keep four (4) other children besides Dejuan. I have been keeping children since March 1999.
On Sunday, Jacqueline called me and asked me would I keep Dejuan for her to go to church. I believed that she called me at 8:00 A.M. I

151

agreed to keep him. She arrived at my house at 10:00A.M.
I had been cleaning and had started to mop when Dejuan got to my house. Dejuan was in the room with my children while I was mopping. I finished mopping and placed the bucket in the kitchen and walked to the laundry room.

Dejuan was behind me when I went in the laundry room and then returned to the livingroom. I walked down the hallway to the bedroom to put away something. Dejuan was behind me and was playing with a pound-a- ball and was standing in the bedroom door. I turned to walk back to the kitchen and Dejuan had put the toy on the floor and I told him to put the toy away, which he did. I returned to the laundry room with Dejuan following.

He then went into the livingroom where my boys had moved the furniture to play limbo. After placing the white clothes in the washing machine I went back to my bedroom and told my husband to get up. I went into the bathroom and was only in there for a minute. As I was walking out the bathroom door I noticed my bedroom door was shut. I do not know how the door got shut. As I was walking from the bathroom I heard my son, Delson knocking on the door, saying that he thought that Dejuan had drowned. I opened the door and ran down the hall, as did my husband. I looked and saw my husband was holding Dejuan. Dejuan was not breathing and I began to perform CPR and told my son to call 911.

I have been keeping Dejuan since he was 2 weeks old and also keep Derrick, his older brother. Derrick comes to my house before and after school, and they are sometimes there until 10:00 P.M.
The bucket is a five (5) gallon bucket that I purchased at Wal-Mart and had about two (2) gallons of water in it and also had Tide and bleach in the water.
END OF STATEMENT

1745 hours
Investigator Roundtree arrived in CID and met with Maria Jones. Investigator Roundtree read Maria Jones written statement and then conducted taped statement consisting of more specific details surrounding the above events. Maria Jones stated that she received her Home Child Care License in March of 1999. Maria Jones stated that she

recently renewed her license for March 2001 to March 2002. Maria Jones stated that she currently cares for four (4) children to include Anthony Boatwright. Maria Jones stated that she has provided care for Anthony Boatwright since he was two (2) weeks old.

Maria Jones stated that the normal schedule in which she cares for Anthony Boatwright is Monday - Friday 0830 hours to 2100 hours Maria Jones stated that she occasionally provides care for Anthony Boatwright on weekends when Jacqueline Boatwright requests her to do so. Maria Jones stated that this morning at approximately 0800 hours Jacqueline Boatwright called her and asked if she cold keep Anthony Boatwright while Jacqueline Boatwright attended church service.

Maria Jones stated that she agreed and Jacqueline Boatwright advised that she would be over at approximately 1000 hours Maria Jones stated that all the other children inside the residence were asleep so she started cleaning up the house. Maria Jones stated that after straitening up the livingroom, she fixed some mop water. Maria Jones stated that she usually mops the floor twice a day, once in the morning and once in the evening.

Maria Jones stated that she always uses the same formula, which consists of two (2) gallons of water, nine (9) ounces of Clorox bleach and a half (1/2) scoop of tide washing powder. Maria Jones stated that shortly after she fixed the mop water, Jacqueline Boatwright arrived with Anthony Boatwright. Maria Jones stated that Anthony Boatwright appeared restless and she began rocking him because she thought he was sleepy.

Maria Jones stated that the rest of the children woke up and Anthony Boatwright walked into their room and began playing. Maria Jones stated that Anthony Boatwright kept going back and forth between her room and the kid's room.

Maria Jones stated that at approximately 1130 hours she advised the children that she was going to mop the floor and not to come into the kitchen. Maria Jones sated that as she was mopping the floor, Anthony Boatwright came into the kitchen and she told him to go back into the room.

Maria Jones stated that she finished mopping the floor and left the water in the kitchen. And returned to her bedroom. Maria Jones stated that her husband was lying in the bed watching TV and she told him to get up so that she could clean up the room. Maria Jones stated that Anthony Boatwright again began playing back and forth between her room and the kid's room and she told Anthony Boatwright that she was going to use the bathroom.

Maria Jones stated that Anthony Boatwright began walking down the hall towards the livingroom where at least three of the five other children were playing. Maria Jones stated that she walked into her bedroom to use the restroom and when she came out she noticed that her bedroom door was closed. Maria Jones stated that her husband was still lying across the bed and she again told him to get up.

Maria Jones stated that she thought to herself as to why the door was shut but at that time the kids rushed in and yelled that Anthony Boatwright had drowned. Maria Jones stated that she and her husband rushed to the kitchen and her husband grabbed Anthony Boatwright form one of the children, gave him to her and she started administering CPR. Maria Jones stated that she told her husband to call 9-1-1 and that she continued CPR until EMS workers arrived.

Maria Jones stated that she was unsure if she had placed the mop back inside the bucket after she finished mopping. Maria Jones insisted that Anthony Boatwright was only out of her sight for a 1 ½ at the most. Maria Jones stated that she was unsure how the bedroom door got closed after she went into the bedroom.

1900 hours
Investigator Roundtree spoke with Department of Family and Children Services representative Mary Duggins in reference to above case. Duggings was briefed on the incident and advised that she would conduct a follow-up investigation on tomorrow.

2345 hours
Investigator Roundtree contacted Dr. Papizan via telephone to check on the condition of Anthony Boatwright. Dr. Papizan advised that there had been no change in Anthony Boatwright's condition.

091001 (Monday)
1100 hours
        Investigator Roundtree arrived at 2608 Lincolnton Pkwy and attempted to make contact with Maria Jones. Investigator Roundtree knocked on the door for several minutes but received no response. Investigator Roundtree called the residence and the answering machine activated and a message was left for Maria Jones to call Investigator Roundtree.

1230 hours
        Investigator Roundtree arrived at MCG PICU and met with the attending physician, Dr. Anthony Pearson-Shaver and Jacqueline Boatwright. Dr. Pearson-Shaver advised Investigator Roundtree away from Jacqueline Boatwright that Anthony Boatwright only had lower level brain activity and if he were to survive his physical injuries his brain activity would not increase.

091101 (Tuesday)
1200 hours
        Investigator Roundtree received a call in CID from Mary Duggins. Duggins stated that Diane Dye of the State Licensing Division had arrived and that they were inquiring if it was O.K. for them to interview Maria Jones regarding the incident. Duggins stated that she would contact Investigator Roundtree at the conclusion of the interview and advise Investigator Roundtree of the results.

1600 hours
        Investigator Roundtree again contacted Dr. Papizan via telephone to check on the condition of Anthony Boatwright. Dr. Papizan advised that there had been no change.

1630 hours
        Investigator Roundtree called assistant DA William Bowcutt in reference to above case. Bowcutt stated that based on the information available, he could not find any felony criminal charge that could be

pursued. Bowcutt stated that in his opinion the only charge that could be pursued may be a Reckless Conduct but thought that would still be stretching the element of "Gross Neglect" which would be required to make said charge.

Investigator Roundtree subsequently briefed Lt. Francisco and Maj. Autry on the status of the above case.

091201 (Wednesday)
1000 hours
    Investigator Roundtree and Lt. Francisco arrived at the DA's Office and met with Danny Craig. Danny Craig was briefed on the above incident and advised that he would review the facts and offer an opinion as to what if any criminal charges could be pursued.

091401 (Friday)
1600 hrs.
    Investigator Roundtree arrived at 2608 Lincolnton Pkwy. and met with Maria Jones, Montaque Jones, Delson Anderson, Dracy Anderson and Demarcos Anderson.

    Investigator Roundtree, subsequently met with Jacqueline Boatwright along with Major Ken Autry. Major Autry advised Boatwright that the Sheriff's Office was prepared to go forward with Criminal Charges in regards to the above incident. Boatwright stated that she had prayed about the incident and vengeance was not in her heart and she did not wish to pursue any criminal charges. Boatwright advised that she only wanted to make certain that an incident of this type did not happen again.

Based on the meeting with Jacqueline Boatwright, the case will be cleared OTHER.

The *2003 Child Care Center Licensing Study* (February 2003) by the Children's Foundation, and the *2003 Family Child Care Licensing Study* (September 2003) by the Children's Foundation and the National Association for Regulatory Administration, provides the following information on States requiring general liability insurance:

General or Professional Liability Insurance Required by State Child Care Licensing Regulations

Child Care Centers (CCC) and Family Child Care Homes (FCC)

Alabama   No insurance requirements for CCC or FCC.

Alaska   No insurance requirements for CCC or FCC.

Arizona   General liability insurance in the amount of $300,000 is required; no requirement for professional liability insurance. Liability insurance required with a minimum limit of $100,000 for FCC.

Arkansas   No insurance required for CCC. Liability insurance not required for FCC, but highly recommended.

California   No insurance required for CCC. Family child care liability insurance alternatives for FCC must be followed:

1)Aggregate amount of $300,000 with at least $100,000 per occurrence; or

2)$300,000 bond (annual aggregate); or
 arising in connection with the FCC home.
3) provider does not own the premises in which care is provided, then the provider must advise the parents that the owner of the property or the homeowner's association may not provide insurance coverage for losses arising in connection with the FCC home.

Colorado General liability insurance is required for CCC only if the center cares for children paid for by the State. Liability insurance required for FCC only if state pays for children.

Connecticut No insurance required for CCC. Liability insurance not required for FCC; vehicles used to transport children must3)   Signed affidavit from each parent acknowledging that provider has neither insurance nor a bond; and

4) If the FC be insured.

Delaware General liability and fire insurance required; if transporting children, auto insurance is required; professional liability insurance is not required. No insurance required for FCC.

District of Columbia No insurance required for CCC or FCC.

Florida   No insurance required for CCC or FCC

Georgia   No insurance required for CCC or FCC.

Hawaii No insurance required for CCC. Liability insurance not required for FCC; providers must inform parents whether it is available or not.

Idaho No insurance required for CCC. FCC not licensed.

Illinois General public liability insurance with $300,000 per occurrence required; professional liability insurance not required. Liability insurance not required for FCC; vehicle insurance is required if transporting children.

Indiana No insurance required for CCC or FCC

Iowa No insurance required for CCC or FCC

Kansas General liability insurance and accident insurance for children is required; if transporting children, vehicle must be insured for $100,000/$300,000 for injury and $50,000 for property; professional liability insurance is not required. Liability insurance not required for FCC; vehicle insurance is required if transporting children.

Kentucky General liability insurance of at least $100,000 per occurrence required; professional liability insurance not required. Liability insurance is required for the FCC provider with coverage of $100,000 per accident

Louisiana   General commercial liability insurance required for Class A licensed centers and vehicles if transporting children; professional liability insurance not required. FCC not licensed.

Maine General liability insurance required; professional liability insurance not required.   No insurance required for FCC.

Maryland   No insurance required for CCC. Liability insurance is required for FCC if the provider's facility is located in an area covered by a homeowner's or condominium association; if it is required, the provider must carry liability insurance for at least $300,000.

Massachusetts   General liability or professional liability not required for CCC. If center transports children, vehicle insurance is required at $100,000/ $300,000 with $5,000 property damage. No insurance required for FCC.

Michigan   No insurance required for CCC or FCC

Minnesota No insurance required for CCC. Liability insurance strongly encouraged for FCC; if provider has insurance less than $100,000 per person and $250,000 per occurrence, or no insurance, written notice of level of coverage must be given to and signed by parents of each child in home.

Mississippi No insurance required for CCC or FCC.

Missouri   No insurance required for CCC or FCC.

Montana   General liability insurance that is considered "adequate" is required; professional liability insurance not required. Liability insurance required by law for FCC, described as "adequate insurance." No specific amount in the Statute.

Nebraska No insurance required for CCC or FCC.

Nevada   General liability insurance to a third person required for CCC; if providing transportation, adequate insurance needed to cover liability for health or injury, medical expenses, damages covered by uninsured motorist; professional liability insurance not required. Liability insurance required to third person for FCC. Bureau must be notified at least 30 days before cancellation or non-renewal of policy.

New Hampshire   General or professional liability insurance is not required for CCC, although programs must disclose to parents, prior to enrolling children, if the program is not covered by liability insurance. Liability insurance required for FCC.. If provider is not covered, must disclose this fact to the parents.

New Jersey General liability insurance required for CCC, no specific coverage amount; professional liability insurance not required; if transporting children, vehicle insurance required in the amounts specified by the Department of Motor Vehicles. FCC not licensed.

New Mexico No insurance required for CCC. Liability insurance not required for FCC, but encouraged.

New York General liability insurance required for CCC; professional liability insurance not required. No insurance required for FCC.

North Carolina No insurance required for CCC or FCC.

North Dakota General liability insurance required for centers and preschools only; professional liability insurance not required. No insurance required for CCC.

Ohio No insurance required for CCC or FCC.

Oklahoma General or professional liability insurance not required for CCC; only transportation medical and liability insurance required. Liability insurance not required for FCC; vehicle insurance is required if transporting children.

Oregon No insurance required for CCC or FCC.

Pennsylvania Comprehensive general liability insurance required for CCC; professional liability insurance not required. No insurance required for FCC.

Rhode Island General liability insurance for personnel, children enrolled and transportation required for CCC; professional liability insurance not required. No insurance required for FCC.

South Carolina No insurance required for FCC.

South Dakota General liability insurance required for CCC; transportation insurance covering passengers required; professional liability insurance not required. Liability insurance not required for FCC, but providers are reminded that their homeowner's policy may require additional amendments when providing a business in the home.

Tennessee General and automobile liability insurance and medical payment insurance required for CCC. Liability insurance coverage shall be maintained in the minimum of $500,000 per occurrence and $500,000 general aggregate coverage. General liability insurance for FCC (minimum $300,000 general aggregate coverage or per occurrence), automobile liability (minimum $300,000 combined single limit of liability) and medical payments coverage (minimum $5,000 for injuries to children being transported and minimum $5,000 for injuries to children resulting from operation of the child care facility) required.

Texas Liability insurance in the amount of at least $300,000 for each occurrence of negligence covering injury to a child while the child is in the care of license holder required. The facility must provide the Licensing Division and parents written notification if liability insurance is unavailable because of financial reasons, inability to find an underwriter willing to issue policy, or the limits of the current policy are expended.
No insurance required for FCC.

Utah No insurance required for CCC. Liability insurance not required for FCC; vehicle insurance is required if transporting children.

Vermont General liability insurance required in an unspecified amount for CCC; if transporting children, property damage, bodily injury and liability insurance required; professional liability insurance not required. General liability insurance required for FCC in an unspecified amount; if transporting children, property damage, bodily injury and liability insurance required.

Virginia General liability insurance required with a minimum of $500,000 each occurrence; if transporting children, must be insured with the minimum limits as established by State statutes; professional liability insurance not required. No insurance required for FCC.

Washington General and/or professional liability insurance not required for CCC.. Proof of liability and medical insurance is required for centers transporting children. Liability insurance not required for FCC; vehicle insurance is required if transporting children.

West Virginia General liability insurance required for CCC; professional liability insurance not required. No insurance required for CCC.

Wisconsin General liability insurance for CCC with a limit of not less than $25,000 each person and a total limit of $75,000 per occurrence; vehicle insurance required when transporting children; professional liability insurance not required. Liability insurance not required for FCC, but parents must be notified.

Wyoming No insurance required for CCC. Liability insurance not required for FCC, but strongly recommended.

Getting a bill passed into law

Many people have asked me about the process of getting a law passed. I can honestly admit it was not easy. Laws are passed because of passion and hard work. If you desire to get a law passed you must understand the political process. I am proof that ordinary folks can be influential in change when they are diligent and relentless in their efforts. The process for ordinary folk who are trying to get laws passed is commonly known as grassroots. Grassroots efforts can include everything from writing letters, picketing, collecting signatures, making media appearances, and the like.

The media can be key to getting your efforts out to the attention of the public by reaching people who might not otherwise know about what you are attempting to do. Hopefully they will see your plight and offer to support you. Keep in mind that everyone is not going to be on your side. However, good publicity or bad publicity can be an asset if used in the proper manner.

The next step is to contact your state or federal representative, depending on which level of the law you desire to change. Your representative will have his legal staff draft the bill. The bill will be given an identifying number and introduced by your representative to the body of government which he or she is a member, whether that be the House or the Senate. From that point on the bill will be known as Senate Bill or House Bill followed by the identifying number. Once the bill has been introduced and has a number you can go online to the state's website or the federal website and keep track on what actions are being taken on the bill. Whichever body introduces the bill, will send it to the appropriate committee for vote.

In the other words, if your bill is introduced by a senator it will go to a senate committee and vice versa. This is the most important part of the process. Most bills never make it out of committee. So don't think just because it has been introduced you are home free to getting a law passed. This is the stage where legislators who are members of the committee decide which bills are going to be sent to the chamber floor for vote. At this point, you need to find out the name of the person who is the chair of the committee and contact their office. In addition, write them a letter and send an e-mail. If you have a personal story associated with the bill, by all means express that to the committee chair. Don't forget to ask to be a speaker at the hearing.

If the bill does get a hearing, the committee will vote right then and there whether or not the bill will go to the floor of whichever chamber introduced it. For purposes of this writing, we will say your bill has made it out of committee and is headed to the floor for vote.

Once on the floor of the House or Senate, again depending on who introduced it, the legislator informs his collegeaues of the bill's language and what purpose it will serve to the benefit of the people. The legislator's colleagues will be given the opportunity to ask questions, state opposing views, and give personal opinions concerning the bill. The chamber leader will ask for the legislators to vote yes or no on the bill. If the majority of the legislators vote in favor, it passes and moves to the opposite chamber for the same process. For example, if it started in the House, it now goes to the Senate for the same process; introduction, committee assignment, committee hearing and vote, and finally to the chamber floor for final vote. Once both chambers floors have favorably passed the bill, it is then sent to the Governor's office for his or her signature or veto.

If the Governor does not veto the bill it automatically becomes law after a certain time period whether he signs it or not.

It may seem like it is a simple process but I can assure you the process is anything but simple. There are many reasons, having little to do with you but everything to do with politics, that can be detrimental to getting a bill passed into law. If the Democrats are in control or are majority in members then they could be the deciding factor the same if the majority of members are Republican. As for me Jesus was always in control and I knew those who were with me were more than those who were with them. Be blessed.

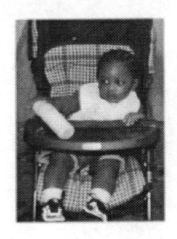

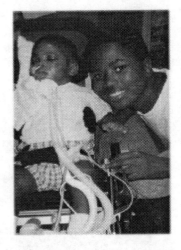

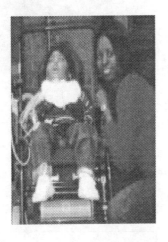

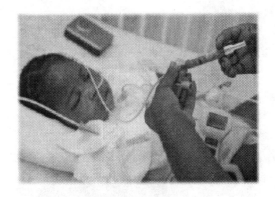

Photos courtesy of
Andrew Davis Tucker
Augusta Chronicle

May the blessing of Jesus Christ rest upon you and your family. Thank you for reading and sharing the Good News.

Jacqueline Boatwright